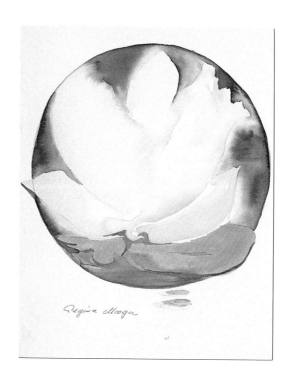

Regina Maga

I KNOW FROM MY HEART

JACK SCHWARZ

CELESTIAL ARTS CA BERKELEY, CALIFORNIA

Cover and text design by Ken Scott
Typeset by Ann Flanagan Typography
Illustrations by Regina Marga

Library of Congress Cataloging-in-Publication Data

Schwarz, Jack, 1924–
    I know from my heart / Jack Schwarz.
        p.   cm.
    ISBN 0-89087-665-7 :
    1. Spiritual life.   I. Title.
    248.4—dc20

                                                                91-38780
                                                                CIP

First Printing, 1992
Printed in the United States of America

    2 3 4 5 — 96 95 94 93 92

To all my fellow beings on the Path of Knowing

ACKNOWLEDGMENTS

My thanks to the teamwork and cooperation that made possible this beautiful book.

My acknowledgment to Regina Marga, Bernice and David Sage, Marilyn Woodward, Kathy and Rick Martin, Bryan Brunzell, Helen Wallace, Tom Luhnow, Deanna Richards, Pat Monroe, Bea and Buddy Frumker, and Alice and Jim Sours for all their caring and sensitivity in preparing this writing. A special thank you to David Hinds and Celestial Arts.

And my gratitude to my wife and partner, Lois, for her steadfast encouragement and joy.

CONTENTS

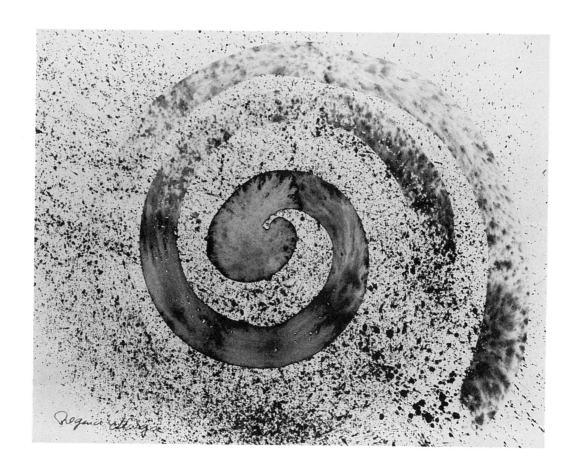

When we arrive in this world,

    Into this life we have been swirled.

Dedicated to health and happiness,

    Nothing more and nothing less.

And very soon we did find out,

    Enhancing and tracking the path was quite a bout.

Searching along till we discover,

    That in this life 'tis good to be the lover.

So, there is no room or place for hate,

    That's why to embracing love we dedicate.

THE BEAUTIFUL LOTUS

From a homely bulb so dull and brown,
  Shriveled and dank with mold,
Sprang a lotus dressed in velvet gown.
  A lotus whose heart was gold.

A bulbous earth of stardust molded,
  Sown to the winds by a flying sun,
Opened its heart and there unfolded,
  A spirit whose feet the stars outrun.

So life, composite of earth and heaven,
  Spawn of the seas and the gods divine,
Of Beauty and Truth and Love the leaven,
  For earth ultimate hope its seal and sign.

Not where the distant suns are grooming
  Their fiery steeds for a farther flight.
But there, where the lotus bulbs are blooming,
  Life's drama rises to a godlike height.

Regina Mooga

ARE YOU READY FOR THE 1990S?

ONGRATULATIONS! YOU MADE IT THROUGH THE EIGHTIES. I have called it the decade of greed. A decade of narcissism. A decade in which we worked to get better for the sake of self only.

We lost sight of what could set us free. We hung on to the past. The past became a tremendous torrent of energy directed upon ourselves. What were the results of this? Not enough radiance! We gave the false pretense that everything was okay. We did not do activities in a sharing process. Therefore, we forced this decade to end with a new uprising for liberty.

Whenever we hold back from things we feel we have a need for, but do not try to acquire them, pressure builds up. Eventually we perceive that we need to do something. We can no longer take it. We must do something about it. This is why the walls came down and are still coming down.

Now we have entered into a decade I am calling the decade of compassion, freedom, and integrity. The decade of wholeness. The decade of healing. Yes, we are breaking the walls down but the chaos has not been removed. That is a very good sign, for it shows us what our next step needs to be.

What have we done to the earth and those who live upon it? What about the surfacing of racism? Now we are recognizing these conditions and can set ourselves free from them. We then can allow the energy to flow freely from ourselves to others. It depends upon the quality we have within us to bring healing about. To heal not only humankind's understanding of its function, but also to heal the earth on which we exist. To bring understanding and to grasp integrity, wholeness, honesty, and the power of love, compassion, and fortitude into an expression in which the earth can restore itself. We will then find the order in the chaos.

We now need to drop our disturbance with the chaos. We now need to say that we have something ahead of us, something to work for. It becomes a decade of building a higher state of our own beingness, to have the chance to obtain the sublime in this life. We will therefore go into the new millennium in a totally different state than we are in now. We have a whole decade for it. I know that all of us are very anxious. We all have felt in the latter months of the last decade the stirring within us. We became aware that we too have been sitting back just allowing these things to happen. We were so interested and so involved in our own development and not willing to work with that development. We wanted to reach "it" very fast. We had blinders on. We only had one goal in mind: "making it."

We missed many things which could give us a better understanding. When we find the new step, we must utilize what we found on that step no matter what it is. By breaking down physical barriers, we open up borders. It continues as a resonance over the whole world, a strong vibration which stirs up even the most stagnant state in our foundations. You need to start activating these three aspects: love, compassion, and fortitude. All three are a necessity for healing, for making things whole.

The first aspect is love, love for the sake of others. Whatever we have done, we need to recycle it and for-give it to the world. Sharing it with others makes love an act of participation. The first ingredient is the necessity to bring this love into an active state for all humankind.

The second aspect is compassion. Compassion cannot come forth unless we first create a desire, a passion, a lust for activity. Compassion does not happen by itself; it is not an act of osmosis. We all have to discover within ourselves this inner desire to participate. Now we must start to heal ourselves for the sake of all humankind.

We will become like suns supplying energy without judgment, without any self-righteousness. That passion becomes a growing state which blooms into a state of compassion. By sharing our passion it becomes compassion. It becomes an outpouring of the heart into the heart of others. You are part of this. We can look each other in the eye and find a kinship, no matter who the person is. We will bow our heads for our children's integrity, for their wholeness. We will no longer suppress or oppress the development of the harmonious state of soul, mind, and body.

That will bring forth the third aspect, fortitude. You have heard the common statement, "I have a lot of intestinal fortitude." Let us make that intestinal fortitude become a very active fortitude so that it goes beyond the gut level. It then becomes a fortitude from the heart, expressed by our wholeness and our readiness.

You know I asked the question, "Are you ready for the 1990s?" Well, if you were not ready, things would not have happened the way they happened. Become aware of this readiness. Start looking for the tools and experience you already have. Start to use them. Do not sit on the curb of the road of life complaining about how bad it was. Now you have the chance to make what was bad into a perfect state.

Every time I perceive this idea, I see how all of us are one with nature. How all of us are acting according to our inner beingness, our totality. Again I see the symbol used throughout the ages: the lotus. How it sets itself free from a decaying bulb. A decaying bulb gives its own energy to the stem, which gives it the capacity to drive itself up through the water, water being symbolic of the emotions. Go through the emotions; do not avoid them. Do not repress the emotion. Freely get the energy into motion and bring it out. Your leaves will spread out over the emotional planes. Then the first bud will appear with the promise of the lotus blossom.

In the heart there is the development of a new level of consciousness. We indeed can become aware that we always were and will be the jewel in the lotus. We have spent enough time on the jewel without becoming aware of the lotus itself. The lotus has a much greater meaning, for the jewel was always there but could not bring out its radiance if the petals did not open. We can open our petals and recognize that these fears which come up to the surface of questioning are an incentive to go on. You cannot become oblivious of the needs. We are now in a state where we have allowed the wounds to open. The poisons will come out. Do not think that just because we have opened the wounds, that now everything is okay.

We need to start looking at what this decade is going to bring. It is the decade of healing that needs to be activated. It is not healed yet. It is time to put down our scalpels and start suturing the wound. We need an ointment of love and compassion so the fortitude will come forth in the process of healing.

How many of us have asked ourselves, "What is my function?" "Why did I come here?" "Why did I choose this planet to be on when I see what we have done to it?" But you know, if it had not been done to this planet, what would your function be, to just enjoy being here and doing nothing? Would you have expected then to grow? Because of the way you were brought into this chaos, you can find the order in it.

Now we have the opportunity to start seeing that each of us has a definite function. We each have an individual need to recognize our function. No matter in which vocation, gender, race, philosophy, or creed, we have to find this oneness.

We have no excuse any longer. The walls are down; the past is free. In front of you there are a lot of bricks lying around. You can either climb over them or just negate and leave them behind, realizing that you leave not only the chaos behind, but also your understanding of what your real function is. All you have to do is start using the bricks to build a new world. Do not leave this one behind, but start to act upon it. Find what your function is no matter how small or large it might seem. It now is indeed one for all and all for one.

It does not mean that suddenly you are going to like the world you see ahead of you. It might mean that you will not like the beings with whom you will need to cooperate. You did not come here to like them or their actions, you came here to learn how to love them.

None of us have made the wrong choice or just haphazardly come about. I really feel and know, and speak from within my own knowingness, that all of you, no matter what you are capable of, no matter what your talents or potential abilities are, are all here to make this new world, this new millennium to come. This brings us to a higher level of consciousness, and therefore a higher level of integrity.

You have been very severe on yourselves, even in your ignorance. Every time you did something which society said was not perfect, boy did you hate it and did you punish yourself for it! In the first place, you thought that what society portrayed as perfect was perfect; so many could not be wrong.

Well, they were wrong about your perfection; they might have been right about their perfection. If that is the path they need to walk, that is the path they need to walk. Eventually, they will see there is something else, that we need to respect the perfection within each of us. In reality, you are saying that they are not portraying your perfection. So there must be something wrong with them, not realizing that it is a mirroring aspect to feel within ourselves that we are aiming at that perfection. It is a continuously growing state. The moment it becomes perfect, it has lost its perfection. There is something still more perfect. That is a marvelous thing to know, for it keeps us going. It makes it possible for us to acquire this fortitude. Nothing becomes perfect unless strength is put into it.

That strength cannot come forth unless we use our integrity to integrate all our attributes. As long as we are still in the maze, not knowing where the beginning or end is, we are continually going around in circles, like a cosmic surgeon unable to find his sutures. The wounds will stay open and they will eventually fester. The time is now. I must start healing myself so I can stimulate others to heal.

We need to throw off our human arrogance and create an integral relationship with our cosmic arrogance. We need to start dropping this idea that we are better than anyone else. We need to start realizing that we are the best we can be. You can affect your environment.

You need to maintain the activity forty-eight hours a day, not a second less, preferably several hours more. Even in our sleep, or so-called sleep, we are still grasping for the new plans and steps to be taken. Never let up on this activity or become satisfied with what has been done. Recognize yes, it was perfect, it was great, but it can still be more and better. We are not talking about more material activity, for that is what got us into trouble.

In this new decade be prepared to do with less in the material world. We need to return a lot to the earth that we so carelessly took from it. Recognize the dominion you were endowed with. We were put here to care for the earth, to share its harvest, not to rape it. When we start healing ourselves and our society or influencing the society to heal itself, we also heal this planet on which we live. We have a target to achieve to make this the decade of healing.

Are you ready for the 1990s? If you are, get going! I know that the universal and the creative forces will be helpful, if you recognize them. See Nature already roaring. It is giving you a little hand in starting to build. You have a comrade in Nature.

I hope every effort you make will eventually become effortless and that this becomes your natural state. Thank you for sharing this with me.

ENERGY

God created the universe full of vitality.

    The creative force, omnipotent, God in all,

That what was, is, and forever will be,

    What we call Cosmic Energy.

The ancient wise and scientists of today,

    They all proclaimed the cosmic law.

Energy not to be created nor destroyed,

    It shows the way of transformation, as they saw.

Einstein dreaming he rode a ray of light,

    Defined energy as mc^2.

He qualified energy as radiant, bright,

    To give us vital insight and make us aware.

Being aware of God's energy in constant change,

    To keep our spirit, mind, and body radiantly clear.

To be co-creative in its greatest range,

    Staying healthy and happy, for change no fear.

BACK TO SCHOOL AND BACK TO WORK

 E ALL NEED TO GO BACK TO SCHOOL AND BACK TO WORK. This is the message of the day. When leaves fall, we gather and then spread them on the earth to make humus, food and nutrition for the earth and ourselves. Back to school means we are arranging a new state of life.

We have come to the last decade of these two millenniums. We are about to enter a new state of consciousness and now, in the nineties, are in the process of entering that state. When we talk about energy, we must realize we mean energy with volution, the spiraling of life. We need to bring ourselves to a new state of values.

Now is the time to look at values. What are the values of the day? When aiming at peace, recognize that qualities of peace are inherent within us. By bringing our excitement into action we achieve harmony, being at peace with each other. We have not yet fulfilled the values of today. Now it is time to go back to school. The new school of life has many different classes to choose from. Choices are sometimes very difficult for us make.

Every day we encounter many diseases which we see around us. We see the harm being done by things we are attracted to, such as drugs. We see this as an evolutionary state; we value instead of evaluate it. This is the reason we need a new state of understanding.

Back to work means we must look at what we have already done, and what our new function of life is going to be. This new function of life needs to be a more spiritual state. Recognize that we have, indeed, the capacity to make changes. All of us are endowed with the marvelous spirit of life, the breath of life by which we give new attention to what we are thinking about.

The word "school" is where we need to start looking. Why are we in school? To be educated? To be educated means to "bring forth." We need to bring forth what is inherently within us. What is within us? The spirit of life by which we can give help to anyone here with us. We are all endowed with this potential. When we do not perceive life in this way, we become fearful of all the changes coming about. We hold on to all that was.

We have graduated from our old school, and are ready to go into the new school to work on new ideas, to bring them forth so we can become more valuable in this life. We are all brothers and sisters with a need to come together for greater enjoyment and brightness in life. We are carriers of light. We do not need to wait until we pass on to a new life. We can bring our state of fulfillment to work in this life. We are, actually, the future.

It says in the Scriptures, "Let them become like children." We are indeed children at all times, and we need to go back to our childlike state. In a childlike state of innocence we do not conjure up all kinds of ideas to make ourselves comfortable. We need to become austere in our beingness. That does not mean we are not allowed to have that which we have a right to. However, it needs to be brought into a state of currency, a state of exchange. Bring all things into the glory of God and let them be of service to all humankind. We need to gather the sheaves. After harvesting, we must bring them into productivity.

When we see the tremendous amount of sickness around us, we must realize that we who are still in a state of spirit and light, can bring and share this with whomever is in need. We have to dig deep into our hearts and find the radiance, the love, and then share it with each other. It is a joyful life, a life which has so many great values which we have overlooked.

Cupid is waiting for us to get into action. We sit and lie back so often, without knowing why we are not at work. We are endowed with a tremendous god given spirit, and we are not acting that way.

Choose new values, new units to learn. The units which say we can bring this life into a better state. This world is a glorious world if we make it so. It has so much to offer. We need to start looking at values and how we have evolved. Indeed, become like the saints which already exist within us. We do not need to wait to be sanctified. We are sanctified every day by our inner being.

3

Our consciousness needs to awaken to the spirit of God, to help those who are still in need. Those who cannot yet take the first lesson. We need to take their hands, bring them onto the path, and guide them into the harmonious state. We must do this by example; not by telling them how but by being a model. Be one who shares his / her life with everything that exists.

We are radiant beings. We need to shine forth this radiance which actually brings forth a state of health, of wholeness. Health is an evolutionary state. The "e" in evolution stands for energy, and volution means whirling, rolling, moving, expanding. We can all expand ourselves. The more we expand, the easier we can overcome all that is against us. These are the challenges of life.

Every day, we are shown challenges. Awaken within the understanding and knowingness that we have the power to overcome all that is seemingly against us. We need to see challenges as lessons. We cannot sit down, feel sorry, and grieve for what we think we missed or have not been able to do yet. We have the ability and availability of these powers.

It says in the Scriptures, "The best is yet to be." The best means best every day. Then we need to let it go because we are going to be even better. When looking for perfection, recognize perfection is always there. We need to work towards perfection. When we find it to be perfect, there is still another path which makes it even more perfect. The mystery God has given us is that we do not really know what perfection is. We are being guided to do our best. We need to be dissatisfied with, and at the same time contented with, whatever we do. We must take joy in knowing we did the best we could for now, knowing we will do better next time.

Back to work means to work on God's path. It is in God's hands. Walk with Godspeed. See with God's eyes. Listen to the heart of the song that says, "You have the ability. Be joyful. Do the best you can. Do not sit down and feel that you have not done what you should have done." That is past and the past matters not. We have the need and the ability to go to a new state, a new school.

4

Kahlil Gibran says it so beautifully in his prose poem from *Thoughts and Meditation*, "A Glance at the Future":

From behind the wall of the present, I hear the hymns of humanity. I hear the sounds of the bells announcing the beginning of prayer in the Temple of Beauty. Bells molded in the metal of emotion and poised above the holy altar—the human heart. From behind the future I see the multitudes worshiping on the bosom of nature, their faces turned towards the East and awaiting the inundation of the morning light, the morning of truth. I see the city in ruins and nothing remains to tell man of the defeat of ignorance and the triumph of light. I see the elders sitting under the shade of the cypress and willow trees surrounded by youth listening to their tales of former times. I see youth strumming their guitars and piping their reeds and the loose tressed damsels dancing under the jasmine trees. I see their husband's men harvesting the wheat, the wives gathering the sheaves and singing mirthful songs. I see the women adorning themselves with a crown of lilies and a girdle of green leaves. I see friendship strengthened between humans and all creatures, and clans of birds and butterflies, confident and secure, winging towards the brooks. I see no poverty, neither do I encounter excess. I see fraternity and equality prevailing among humankind. I see not one physician, for everyone has the means and knowledge to heal themselves. I see no Priest, for conscience has become the High Priest. Neither do I see a lawyer, for nature has taken the place of the courts and treaties of amity and companionship are in force. I see that man knows that he is the cornerstone of creation and that he has raised himself above littleness and baseness and has cast a veil of confusion from the eyes of the soul, this soul now reads what the clouds write on the face of heaven and what the breeze draws on the surface of the water, now understands the meaning of the flowers' breath and the cadences of the Nightingale. From behind the wall of the present, upon the stage of coming ages, I see beauty as a groom and spirit as a bride.

5

I think he says it so beautifully; for we are in the process of becoming whole, capable of healing ourselves. By making appropriate decisions we will not need courts and lawyers. We need to see that we now have a brotherhood and a sisterhood awakening to the greatest state of companionship with all nature. The future is here now. We have to work with it and toward it.

THE ENTHUSIAST

When the morning light awakes me and strokes my face,

I know a new life has now begun.

Leaving the past like night behind, I join the race.

Gathering energy from the brightly shining sun,

Overcoming fears of shadows cast.

Oh, how these new ventures do appeal!

Empowered by energy liberated from the past,

Inspired by thoughts which give me zeal.

They broaden my horizons, they make me grow.

The victory of truth I know will last.

I now sign my actions as "the Enthusiast."

SPIRITUAL REFLECTIONS

THINK OF SPIRITUAL REFLECTIONS AS DAILY ACTIVITIES, THE SO-CALLED STRUGGLES OF LIFE WITH WHICH WE ARE SO BUSY. When we overcome obstacles with zeal, we sometimes do not take the time to reflect. In Buddhism, for example, a disciple asked his master how to reflect upon life. The master replied that there were five types of reflections or meditations. The first meditation is the meditation of love, in which you must adjust your heart so that you long for the health, wealth, and welfare of all beings, including the happiness of your enemies. That is one of the most important meditations.

We are talking about universal love, the expression of our own inner being. Recognize that when we love these enemies (those who have seemingly sinned against us), we actually cause within ourselves our own inner enemy to speak up. What we think of others is, in reality, the state of our own being. We need to reflect upon why we perceived them as enemies.

When we start working on love for others, we also work on the greatest enemy we will encounter in our life: the "I" self, the ego. We feel as if we are affected by what others have or have not done, especially when they did not do it the way we would have loved or wanted them to do it. In most cases, this is only to achieve a state of self-satisfaction.

Too many times we feel animosity within our hearts for those who are not willing to confirm us. We constantly advertise, rather than reflect. We advertise what our desires or needs are. Then we speak out with fervor that "this is the way it is," not realizing we are sharing it for confirmation that we are right.

If others do not agree with us it is not that they do not want to understand but because they perceive a different truth. Their response should actually awaken a spark within us to reflect upon. Recognize that we must take in all kinds of perspectives and not just those from our own thinking process.

8

When we understand the need to reflect upon our own inner truth, we will recognize that it is our own truth, which can always be expanded upon. There is no need for confirmation when one has enough faith in one's own actions and understanding. The interrelationship of the aspects of your higher self is the source of your information, articulation, and activities.

The second meditation or reflection is the meditation of pity, in which you think of all beings in distress. Vividly present your imagination with the sorrows and anxieties of others so as to arouse a deep compassion for them in your soul. Here at Aletheia we are involved in the so-called "healing process," in making things whole. I have found no better way to self-heal than to put my attention on those who are in a greater state of sorrow and need; those afflicted by life to the extent they cannot function or express their total beingness.

By paying attention to those in greater need, I awaken within myself zeal and enthusiasm, and realize that I have the power to bring out these qualities and reflect them upon others so they may become radiant beings. I am capable of awakening within them their own healing state.

In directing that attention, that energy at others, I do not diminish my own needs. Rather, I share my needs by not giving them the power of self-attachment but instead, I direct that energy at those who seem to be in greater need. When this takes place, we overcome the pity we had for self. It is so easy to become attached to the sorrows and ailments which affect us every day. In many cases, we use them as an excuse for not taking appropriate action. They hold us back in our daily activity.

We often create excuses not to act. It always comes into my mind that, whenever we excuse ourselves, at the same time we accuse ourselves. The French say, "Qui s'excuse, s'accuse," meaning, he who excuses himself, accuses himself.

We see by this second reflection that we need to put all our energy and attention to the needs of our environment. This gives us a better understanding of how we are given dominion over this earth and everything on it. It also means that we must have pity for those aspects which fall within the different kingdoms: mineral, vegetable, animal, and human. We need to develop a greater understanding that the environment needs healing, too. It needs to be made whole again.

9

The third meditation or reflection is joy. With the first two reflections we have acquired a certain state of joy. Whenever we radiate the capacity to overcome pity and to express love, joy surfaces as a result.

In reflecting joy, you think of the prosperity of others and rejoice in their accomplishments. Many prosperity courses are taught which are only directed toward enriching oneself with worldly wealth. I, too, want to become much more prosperous than I have ever been because I know that the more I can gather of these worldly goods, the more material I will have to share and to serve others.

To become prosperous just for one's own sake, however, does not have the aspect of joy in it. It only activates the aspect of greed. The more we have, the more we become afraid of losing. When we get and immediately share or put into the service of others, we immediately see a result.

We are the most blessed people for we have already taken the first step to nonattachment. We need to realize that, in our last days we do not leave anything behind and we do not take anything with us except what we have accomplished in our level of consciousness during this life.

I have stated that I feel blessed because I had the opportunity to start from scratch again. I had no worldly possessions except myself, that which I represented as a physical being. What a fantastic challenge not to have to worry about them anymore or about something happening to them. Not to have to think that somebody else used them and not the way I would have. Look at how stuck we are sometimes in our possessions.

Our joy comes from the opportunity to show others that we can accomplish something when we have a greater understanding of its value. This shows a reflection of our values. What do we put the greatest value on? Look at the purpose the object has. When an object gives you joy, share this joy with others. Reflect joy in your daily life. You will then have a wealth and richness of health accomplished within yourself. This is a spiritual reflection of your total being and not only of your physical aspect.

The fourth reflection is of impurity. In order to understand what is impure, we first need to check within ourselves for what our own truth and purity is. Within ourselves is the causation of all self-righteousness and judgment. We often become very punitive in our expressions and perceive others to be more impure than we are. We achieve this pious state by feeling that what we are and do is always better than what we see in our environment.

We ought not sit in judgment of what others do, even if we do not like their actions. They may still have to fulfill those actions in order to learn from their lessons. I do not have to include myself in actions which I find to be impure. Through reflection upon my own purity, I give greater freedom to my environment and share the energy I release to help others perceive their own state of purity.

When we speak about evil we must realize the greatest evil lies in our judgment, not in what is done by others. We must recognize that wherever corruption occurs, we will not become involved or corrupt ourselves if we do not sit in judgment of it. We should direct our love, happiness, and health to those who, in our perception, are in a state of corruption. Realize that the pleasures of the moment diminish the overall pain of any situation. The moment we live it and have a proper judgment of ourselves, we know how to act and respond to things happening in our life and surroundings.

The fifth reflection is that of serenity. After the four reflections it is time to go within ourselves, into a state of serenity. To some extent, we have taken care of the most important aspects of our lives. We rise above love and hate, tyranny and oppression, wealth and want, to a state of impartial calmness and tranquility. When you have taken care of these other reflections, you have taken care of your daily business.

It is necessary, even in the greatest state of activity, to maintain this state of serenity, of calmness and peace within. This can only happen when in a state of nonattachment. We can be fully, actively involved and deal with the problems, animosities, and necessary struggles of life if we maintain a state of inner peace and knowing. We must act according to our soul's capacity for a life of joy because we know that, whatever happens, we always come out in a higher state of being.

Recognize that everything goes in cycles and what goes around, comes around. What goes up comes down. Neither of these stages is better than the other. Many times, going down is the starting point of the return to higher levels. There is no reason to suddenly feel that we are now in a state we do not deserve. Therefore, do not stop the momentum of moving forward in every direction toward a greater state of serenity and knowingness. We will then accomplish the function for which we came onto this earth. Particularly in providing good governing over the dominion we were given.

Those are the reflections I wanted to share with you for they are a tremendous aspect of every part of our lives. They are reflections which need to occur at any given moment when we feel stagnant and distraught and are not able to foresee what to do. Many times we plan and are so structured in our plans that we fail to act upon our spontaneity, not realizing that our life is in a constant state of change.

We need to be very flexible in our reflections so that we know we will be ready for whatever change may occur.

COURTEOUS

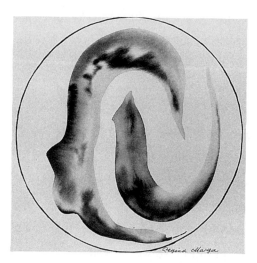

When the Sunday morn has passed,
    All too often a cloud is cast.
And forgotten seems the devotion,
    Of joy and love no more notion.
Back into our daily life,
    Full of obstacles and strife.
This is why we ask,
    Isn't spirituality a full-time task?
Therefore let us see it as a fact,
    That courtesy is a spiritual act.
It means consideration for others,
    Affable to our sisters as well as our brothers.
Our love of Sundays sustained,
    Throughout our life respect for all maintained.

FOUNTAINS OF THE MIND

FOUNTAINS OF THE MIND. ARE WE TALKING ABOUT FOUNTAINS OF THE MIND OR JUST ONE PART OF THE MIND? This so-called "lower" mind, the "I" mind, in which we are so involved in the personal self, is only one part of the mind. It is not the perception of higher spirituality. The feeling of spirituality brought forth in every aspect of our lives includes the fountains of the lower mind.

We can get upset with our environment and ourselves because we still feel we are digging in the mud. While we are digging, we bring up fountains of stuff and spray the rest of the world with it. Do not forget that beauty comes forth out of the process of decay. We should not be too upset with the fountains because they make us aware that there is also a restraining action which restrains us from the truth. It restrains us from "the windows of pure perception." When we become aware that we are spreading this fountain of the deep lower mind into our environment, we become aware that we are affecting it in a way that is not directed toward our spirituality. We could say that we have no excuse for allowing these fountains of the deep unless they result in something beautiful coming forth.

I am always reminded of how the lotus, a symbol in many schools of thought, represents the most beautiful state of being, the highest level of perception. I think the observance of the lotus is marvelous. We sometimes have moments when we are lotus-like; we open our petals and shine our integrity into this world. We sometimes forget how we got these perceptions; how this beautiful flowering state of our being came about. It was part of the fountains of the deep. You stirred them up in order to get the changes going.

It does not mean that we can excuse ourselves; instead, it means we need to keep the awareness that the lotus came forth out of a bulb planted in the mud, deep in the soil. Through the process of decay, it sprouts and the stem rises through the water, through emotions. Realize that these emotions, our physical selves, stir up muddy areas, our sewage area, you could say. From this state of decay we begin to realize that we are not only physically, but also mentally and spiritually constipated.

We need to activate from above, to startle and release. When the process of decay is changed into emotion, energy gets into motion. It comes upward, actually driving through the stem of your being, reaching your receptive heart. This open the windows of your soul. Transmutation of those aspects you do not like about yourself takes place. It is a matter of growth. It is a matter of maturing.

This flowering state is constantly fed by the releasing aspect of decay, which we call transmutation. We need to be in that process. We should not be too hard on ourselves and try to hold it back. As long as you do not work with it, your flower will not be visible. You will just have a stem going through your water. It is when it has received its capacity to transcend the decaying process that the greatest beauty comes. It is uplifted by the light that shines. Suddenly you realize the restrained truth is now clear.

It awakens you to become a radiant being, a healthy being. We can even translate it into the physiology of our bodies. The process of decay, of change, takes place all the time, twenty-four hours a day. Do not be fearful of that and repress it, not showing the outer world what you are and letting them know what process you are going through. Do not have expectations. Know you are finally making an effort to let this come through. Our buds are nourished by what we release, what we were repressing.

14

The fountains of the deep now become the fountains of joy and happiness. They are not operating down in the deep anymore but have arisen to a higher state of being. Then the flower opens up and rests its petals upon its green leaves, giving you balance, stabilizing your life, no longer teeter-tottering. You are no longer thinking, should I or should I not express myself as I am? You will express yourself by your beingness, not by your words, every moment of your life.

We seem to be slightly ashamed to show our spirituality and so hold back our radiance. To affect others with this radiance is your god given gift. It is within your capacity to be the self-healer. Thereby, you heal your outer environment. It has to come from the fountains of the deep. If you do not stir them, your flower will not bloom. We must realize that beauty is hidden deep within our lower mind. Your lower being, your "I" self is the vehicle used to show the spiritual prophet.

In autumn, the leaves start to fall and everything looks barren; however, there is still new growth. Nature takes a rest to bring the seeds back into action. It is time for us to plant the bulbs. They will be lightly covered by the snow of life, and invisible. Remember that the snow, this coolness, at the same time helps the bulbs maintain warmth to grow. It activates the fire within to get through the process of decay, bringing forth a beautiful flowering state when spring recurs.

Remember, you go through four seasons every year. But every twenty-four hours you also go through the four seasons. Every day you have your spring; every day you have your summer in which you become fruitful. You will see a harvest. Every day you go into fall to rest, to prepare to make your harvest productive the next day. Then you have winter, which you call night. After going through three seasons that day, you deserve to rest. Make sure these are restful nights, not a tossing and turning about in your fountains of the deep. Is this wintertime not the time that the snow needs to cool the heat of the fire, thereby maintaining the fires so that spring arrives with morning?

You are born again into a new life. Even your flower, which started to wither slightly, has immediately gotten new life and started to bloom again. Each new day is such an exciting moment. You will still go through ups and downs. That is what the cycle of life is all about.

In the Scriptures, it says in Gen. 8:2, "The fountains of the deep and the windows of heaven also were stopped and the rain from heaven was restrained." When the fountains of the deep started to come up, we were suddenly blinded: rain, truth, as it came down from heaven, was restrained. Restrained, not stopped. The truth did not stop. It was restrained. It closed the windows of our perception of that truth. We now need to make the fountain capable of rising from the deep into a higher state. The truth can mingle, integrate, and merge with us so that it is felt within the heart.

In Proverbs it says, "When He made from the skies above, the fountains of the deep became strong." These fountains of the deep became strong because they were not held back. We sometimes stop the fountains by hiding them and trying to bring them down because we are not supposed to have them. This is like saying, "We are not supposed to have night. We are not supposed to have darkness. We are not supposed to have shadows."

How would you know what life was all about if not for the shadows? How would you know truth, if not for the untruth? How would you ever recognize love if you did not, from time to time, feel a little swelling of envy and jealousy to make you aware that you were not acting in an appropriate way? You have to find that joy again because the opposite aspect hurts. It is painful. These are the pains of life we need to go through to become aware that, from suffering, joy is born. We did not cause the suffering but were suffering from our ignorance.

By setting free the pains we become aware of the truth and of our capacity to be radiant, flowering beings; to be a lotus. Your soul is that jewel. The jewel exists within the lotus. The Buddha constantly reminds himself of the changes in these fountains of the deep and the need to keep focussing upon the jewel which comes forth out of it.

16

The chant, "O mani pahdmi om," means "Oh, beautiful jewel in the lotus." This is not just for a particular religion. It is a way of life. It is not stuck in dogma or doctrine. It is enhanced by our actions. It is our beingness which counts. Religion means togetherness, not a dogma or doctrine. It does not mean you should and should not. It means you need to be aware of your endowment and purpose in life, and to bring these together. Enjoy the flowering state, but, at the same time, share it with others. It is a matter of relating, of sharing everything of your being with everyone else. That is what life is really all about, in my perception.

I am not saying to you, "This is the way you have to be." I am pointing out to you what I have discovered for myself every day, and now I share it with you. I cannot repress my fountains of the deep. Sometimes I mutter and squawk and do all kinds of strange things. Sometimes I throw drops of mud on others. Immediately, though, I put my awareness into action and say, "Now let me make changes." I must not sit in the corner sucking my thumb feeling guilty; that is repression. Repression makes you less radiant. Repression makes us "mal at ease." The French call it "malady." We call it disease. Recognize that, yes, you are perfect but you need to bring this perfection out. In going through the process of discovery, act upon what you have discovered. Do not hold it back; bring it out. There will be times that you will not be liked very much. Do not forget that, in order to be liked, you need first to like yourself.

Each day perhaps, we should make a statue, chiseling away at whatever is excessive and unnecessary until we discover moments of beauty and grace. Then we will indeed have conquered the fountains of the deep.

LIFESTYLE

A lifestyle portrays the way we live,

　　Displaying to what importance we give.

Remember, we have the option of which style to choose,

　　Determining what to gain and what to lose.

If the style has happiness in its pursuit,

　　Active spirituality needs to be the root.

The joy of serving for the benefit of all,

　　Prevents a fast rise and an even faster fall.

Through sacrifice we measure gain,

　　Happiness and integrity we maintain.

Even though the future seems sometimes frail,

　　A spiritual lifestyle keeps us on our trail.

Be aware of the truth we all know,

　　We always reap what we sow.

THE POLARITY OF NEGATIVE AND POSITIVE

THE POLARITY OF NEGATIVE AND POSITIVE ENHANCES NEARLY EVERY ASPECT OF OUR LIVES. Recognize that the universe was created by the creative force—God—as a bipolar energy field. It continuously moves from the positive into the negative and from the negative into the positive. This does not mean that either is good or bad.

By misunderstanding good and bad, we give more value to one than to another. As I perceive it, the purpose of our lives is to be involved with the growing part, to reach back to the state from which we originated; as light beings coming forth out of the dark.

Being brought into the light to manifest the polarity is an indication of the state of harmony. When we involve this "positive" action, we draw in energy and begin to create. Involvement means taking in ideas and putting them into action. It is what stimulates an evolutionary state, the state of growth. We achieve a state where we become aware of the need to let go of that which has already fulfilled its function. The energy needs to be set free to be brought into a new state.

Look around the world and see the amount of things not functioning well. In most cases we have not evolved into awareness of the transformations which took place. This causes a state of unease within our whole being. We want to expand what we experience rather than maintain forms.

Whatever affects us physiologically will immediately affect us mentally. The reverse is also true. The mind is the directive that activates the body and maintains that activation. We stagnate whenever we hold on to the past. Many of us do not involve ourselves in the present when we look at the future and do not know what it will bring. Our experiences may not have been so good when we had them, but now we call them good. We do not understand that it is a process of perceiving and expressing.

20

When we look at our society, we see all kinds of set rules giving us indications of what we need to change. Things are set to direct you in your behavior and put you in specific situations. The challenge is for us to begin to express rather than repress and withdraw just because we do not know what the result from this activity will be.

We still perceive by maintaining the idea of good and bad, not realizing that a process of harmony must occur. Do not identify things as good and bad but rather as contracting and expanding, taking in but immediately activating and expressing, setting free, giving out. We allow our "behavior modifying" society to put certain pressures upon us to behave in this or that way. We misunderstand that lack of expression stagnates our process. It should challenge our process.

We have a tendency to complain that society should behave this or that way, more fitting, in our perception, to our own being. We try to change everything on the outside. Not only do we want to change the outside, but we also want to be in charge of that change.

Rarely do we learn anything, because we are not involved in the process. We give it over to those who have directed us to be a certain way. And now we want them to change rather than changing and adapting ourselves. We need to adapt, not to others' patterns, but to our own perceptions of how we choose to live. We have the option to live by either expressing, or by only taking in and never giving out. Check within yourself how expressive you are. Do not see expression purely as verbalizing. If, at this moment I were only expressing words, they might sound very hollow to you.

If I cannot put my whole inner being into expression, then my energy is not being set free to touch and affect everything in my environment. The fire in me brings up an urge to relate and communicate, not only with words, but with my whole beingness. Start seeing this relationship, because it stirs and activates your inner being too. No matter how you judge or evaluate what I say, always check the immediate stirring in your mind which activates your desire to relate.

The relationship of polarity occurs when the positive attracts the negative and the negative attracts the positive. It begins creating a beautiful state of harmony. Even though we may not be in agreement in words or the manner in which we express ourselves, as long as the energy harmonizes, we still create a relationship which brings convergence. My daily experiences and the letting go of them gives me a greater capacity to understand my values and how I respond to them. In this way, I avoid judging others who live differently than I do.

We have to look again to the root. What are the lessons which have to be learned? They test us on the status of our own inner harmony. Harmony only comes from within. You can be treated by anyone in any mode, method, or form, but unless you involve yourself in the process, you will not grow, evolve, or transcend that state of stagnation.

Every time you make a choice, it is a challenge to check within yourself how much value you put on the pursuit of happiness. It is a fascinating, expressive life in which we are constantly stimulated to action, without looking in advance for the gain. Every day is a day of surrender, a surrendering of the "I" self to the "Thou" self. The "I" self tries to maintain a certain status, even though, within itself, something says, "Move on. Drop the old clothes and get into new ones." I am talking about your radiance in which you are cloaked. Your own being does not stop at your skin.

It is a matter of starting to love harmony. The word "philosophy" is so fantastic. Love is philos and wisdom is sophia. Philos is the masculine part and sophia is the feminine part. The forming part is philos (love) and the expansive, expanding, resonating part is sophia (wisdom). When we bring out that harmony, we use the word in a different way. We have orchestras which play philharmonically, having love of harmony. Life is like playing in an orchestra, one in which we are not only the musicians but also the conductor. We need to make sure that harmony, the polarity between the positive and negative, is maintained. There is a synthesis taking place; all are working together.

Scientists have found that conductors of philharmonic and symphony orchestras live longer. Besides living longer, they also live happier and healthier lives and their immune systems function very well. By constantly conducting, their left and right brain operate in synchronicity, allowing them to maintain a higher state of radiance. Being so involved in bringing the music into beingness, their whole system starts working in harmony. They conduct harmoniously; none of the players are out of sync.

We need to look at synchronization, polarity. We can become the conductors of our own lives by seeing everyone in our life as playing their own instruments to their own capacity and ability. We can influence this by the way we conduct our lives; by how well we bring forth the polarity of positive and negative, contraction and expansion.

I cannot understand how knowing this does not excite you! Every day when you get up in the morning, you have already been through a state of polarity because the darkness is gone and its opposite has come forth. Polarity occurs from awakening until sleep, and both need to be in harmony.

If you go through sleepless nights because you are still in the day state, you know that you have problems. You also know that you have not done anything about them. You did not trust your inner knowing that the hours of rest are the time to harmonize, to again become one with the "I" self and the "Thou" self. When this occurs, we need to surrender our lower self, our "I" self, to the "Thou" self where no personality aspects are involved any longer. Only the spiritual "Thou" self gives direction to your beingness.

When you wake up in the morning, you are indeed a new being. You allowed synchronization to take place. Become expressive in every form; do not hold back. Recognize that all the things which seemingly oppose you only occur to startle you to harmonize with them.

I looked forward to the beginning of the 1990s. Nineteen ninety-one was a year of opportunities. In society, things are going in a very fast rhythm. We are experiencing very fast ups and very fast downs. The ups and downs are pretty similar to each other. Our daily lives are the same way. In order to have harmony, we need to understand the rhythm of life. Do not get depressed because today does not seem to be as great as yesterday. Do not lose your momentum of harmony.

When you are up and have a beautiful view of the future, you do not realize that, even though it took a lot of effort to go up the hill, the moment you are on the top, you start going down. This creates the momentum to take a higher step, a higher climb. Do not feel disturbed when things do not go exactly the way you want. Whatever happens to you is part of that process. It is an opportunity to learn things you never knew existed. You are constantly being confronted with new aspects of life. It is the greatest way of achieving and entertaining a higher state of being.

Polarity comes from responding with our hearts, rather than just with our thoughts, and allowing others to be different than we are. Never forget that even in polarity, there is uniqueness; each of us has the opportunity to find our own path. This may be similar to someone else's, but never the same. Therefore, we cannot compare ourselves, our activities, actions, philosophies, thoughts, or feelings with others. We can resonate with them. We can be in harmony with them even though there are differences.

Friends say, "Vive la difference!" It will be marvelous when we realize that though we are all different, together we form a unity. Diversity in unity and unity in diversity. We are all part of this great process of universal life that directs us to a higher state of beingness. When we finally close our eyes, we close this chapter and new life sprouts forth in a different state, maybe even a different form. Is that not a state to become excited about instead of fearing? Is it not good that you went through school, graduated, and can now start practicing what you studied for? It is marvelous that we can look for a new school if we feel we still need to know more. Isn't every day a school day?

Your whole life is a continual learning process, learning to harmonize and understand the purpose of our beingness in this world. We are learning to surrender to our changing needs and to let go of things we thought we needed but found that, by hanging on to them, no renewal took place. It is a state of starting to process and live. This is the path of action in a state of nonattachment.

Learn to let go of that which no longer has any use, even though there is still some feeling for it. We need to set it free. This means we have to let go of yesterday. It will never come back again. Remember that. There is never such a thing as yesterday. There is never such a thing as tomorrow. Whenever it becomes tomorrow, it is only now, again. When it was yesterday, it was now. So we might as well just pay attention to now. Be here now.

Harmonize and polarize your positives and negatives. I think this is a marvelous way to move on and not stagnate. The rewards are so phenomenal we will not pay much attention to all the symptoms. We will not get up in the morning counting our symptoms. We will get up in the morning counting our blessings. Maybe you have a little headache or your back hurts slightly. Notice that your back is hurting, but say, "Wow! My back is hurting slightly but my legs and fingers are still moving very well and my mind is still working fine. My tongue is still moving; my nose is still smelling; my ears are still hearing; my skin is still sensitive. So what if I have a slight backache!" If you activate the rest of your body you should not have much trouble with the back again. It should restore itself. Do not emphasize or announce that you have a backache, or say, "Boy! Do I have a headache! Do I have this or that!" This is advertising your ache and is an avoidance of action.

I am known for voluntary controls. This gives some people the idea that nothing physiologically ever happens to me, and that I am immune to pain and disease. Well, it just so happens that I did a little too much once, did not pay enough attention to my physical body, and I picked up a stomach virus. I had committed myself to go to Washington and give a course. So I went with the virus to Washington. The moment I entered the building and stood in front of the people, there was no virus left because I had no time to put effort—energy—into the virus. I was not going to make friends with it whatsoever or use it to stay away from my commitment.

I had an inner commitment, not so much to the people, but to myself. I said I was going to be there and give the most perfect class possible. Of course, it was the most perfect class I have ever given which is not good enough for the next one. The moment I got in front of the group, my fever and stomachache were gone. The virus was conquered. I did not give it a chance to be victorious over me.

All of us have this inner ability to recognize the different stages we need to go through. You can do all these marvelous things, but you also need to recognize when and when not to act. You see, my ego was actually a little stuck. Everyone thinks that I can do these things without any problems and here I just had a problem. That is why I admit and share it with you.

It is not that we all have achieved it already. It is constantly keeping an eye on what we need to surrender to our highest need. My highest need was to fulfill my service. That, then, made me more excited, got the energy going and made it radiant. Now, in that higher state of energy, no lower energy can penetrate or have power over me. I think all of us can do this if we count our blessings and not our symptoms. We will then have polarity of the positive and negative.

ABUNDANCE

Oh how glorious it is to know,

 We have an abundance of spiritual seeds to sow.

An abundance of tools from the moment of birth,

 To plant our seeds for the enrichment of earth.

An abundance of earthly fruits, the source, the above,

 To express in this world with an abundance of love.

Sharing your abundance, the glorious gifts of life,

 With the power of faith and the departure of strife.

So let us be thankful for this abundance of grace,

 And serve with our souls till the end of our days.

· 5 ·

THE MASTERY OF LIFE

W E HAVE SUCH A LIFE OF ABUNDANCE, PARTICULARLY OF FREEDOM. Up to now, however, it has not been a freedom "for" but rather, a freedom "from." I think a new spark has been lit within us. We can see that we have let go of our need for freedom "from." There is now an abundance of freedom "for." We have the capacity to master this freedom in life.

Each of us is endowed with the qualities of a master. We have misunderstood this aspect. The new idea of freedom "for" does not mean being master over anyone. We have the potential to be master of our own life, to bring it forth into the world. Through self-mastery we develop an empowering rather than overpowering quality.

In the Scriptures, Jesus said, "Ye can do the things I do and even greater things ye can do." This is the most beautiful idea and promise—a promise that has already been fulfilled. When we look within ourselves and become secure with what we know, we bring it out in the full glory of our beingness. We are, then, marveling and empowering our total environment.

There is not a spark radiating from you that does not affect the whole universe. Every action done through self-mastery totally negates anything that is against you. You must realize that whenever anyone makes an effort to offend you, it is only your ego that can be offended. Your knowingness, your mastery, will help you overcome the ego. Every time someone attempts to enter your life, your "take offense" response may be a cry for help from you to you. If you can realize that concept, then also understand what is meant when we say "turn the other cheek." That does not mean to lower ourselves to their needs but rather raise them out of their needs and supply them with that which we have already mastered.

The beauty lies in the knowledge that we can do this every second of our life. We have the ability to recognize that, if we are masters of ourselves, then we already have the power of healing within us. We are, then, all healers. We are all masters. Through our beingness, healing takes place without needing to have the idea that, "I'm healing this, or I'm healing that." Your whole life is being mastered and is an expression of making things whole, of healing.

When you are in the presence of a need, you do not need to know what the need is, because your energy will lift the need up. You will break through all barriers holding you back. It is only when you do not recognize your self-mastery that you become arrogant. You become arrogant when you discover something you think is better than what someone else does. Once you reach self-knowingness, this mastery of life, there is not anyone or anything that can disturb your knowingness. You actually let go of, give away, the idea of having to "believe" it. It is a lower level of belief that is not based upon faith. Faith is based upon knowing.

Jacob Burn wrote six points of faith, six different levels of faith. Many believe that if we just sit and wait, then something in our environment will activate and things will be all right. Many times our prayers are directed this way and become prayers that are affirmations of our disbelief. If we really had faith and knew, we could just send our prayer out and say, "This is what will be done." Then we could let it go, be ourselves, and become the activators of what needed to be done. The prayer then becomes a way of saying, "Thank you, for it *is* already."

It is the constant recognition of what we need to know, what we have mastered, and what we still need to master. Every day becomes a challenge to discover something we have not yet known or realized that we were already masters of. Welcome every challenge, rather than saying, "Everything is so quiet and calm around me." Quite often we are not willing to look at what challenges us, so we miss it.

In society, we are just now awakening to a state of consciousness in which we realize that mastery over others only brings illness, a malfunction of life, and not much peace or harmony. We are just learning to say, "We had better start looking at what we have done up till now."

Even though Jesus said, "Ye can do the things I do and greater things can ye do," how far have we gotten doing the things he did? Have we recognized that we have the healing power within us? Greater things will come when we recognize the things which we already have the capacity to master. There is room and space. Today! Every second of our life!

There is no better school than the school of life. You do not get a Ph.D. from it, but your experiences are your qualifications of mastery. You must realize and understand that a piece of paper is not sufficient to tell you that you are a master of this or that. "By their fruits, will ye know them." Those who can, stand and be radiant. Show your power from within to be and radiate with others, rather than being distressed when someone does something which seems better than what you did. Instead of feeling envy and jealousy, recognize that they are showing you another page in your book of mastery.

Become competitive with yourself, not with or against others. You need to become competitive with yourself in order to reach an understanding of the mastery you already have. You need to reach an expression and knowingness of this mastery. Then realize that you have become self-competitive. You can then say, "This was good, but not good enough. This feels good, but not good enough." In the Scriptures it says, "the best is yet to be." It does not say what the best is or will be. If you knew, you would be satisfied too quickly and would stop. You would have no activity anymore.

It is the constant wanting to know, how can I do it better? This way, you will not count your symptoms any longer, but will count all your blessings. You are not going to get upset with an internal tool that may fail, or be painful sometimes. You will recognize that tool is only one small tool in comparison with all the other tools still available to you. We get so stuck in one thing that did not go right. We create a wall of guilt rather than say, "Hey, I did it wrong again." (Admit it to yourself.) "Now, I have a chance to do it better."

Recognize that every part of the process of healing is also a process of not being at ease. I see so many people who proclaim a certain mastery of life, yet still complain about every little thing that does not go right in their lives. Only through falling, do we learn how to walk. Yet people despise falling, instead of being grateful they can walk. I do not count the times any longer that I fall on my snoot. Often, when I fall, I say, "Wow! It is so fantastic that I, when very young, learned to get up and walk again." With every little pain, I say, "Thank you for making me aware that I am in disharmony." Not because I am in such a bad state.

Many times, people ask me, "Jack, how are you today?" My standard reply is, "For the state I am in, quite well." I recognize there are states indicative of a better state. They are the warning signs. When people say, "What are your credentials?" I know that the best school is the school of life. It is the suffering from life experiences that makes us well. It gives us the joy of today.

Think about all the worries you have had as far back as you can remember. Realize that 99.8 percent of all those worries never came about. Of the approximately ⅕ percent of the worries that did come about, you overcame them, for you are well and here now. You would not be if your worries had really done to you what you were so worried they would do. Every time it seems to be dark around you, just one little spark, one little photon, needs activating to make it bright again. Every time you think you have not got it, something happens. This is the beauty of the universe. Something happens to give you another spark of hope, mastery of self.

Think about all the miseries in your accounting book. You know, in reality, we have been poor accountants rather than master accountants. Our expenditures are viewed as the most important items to jot down. Rarely do we ever jot down our income. We are so afraid we might have to pay a price for this income. We emphasize all those things which we have to pay for in this life, not realizing there are hidden profits in it. The hidden profits are that you begin to discover you are the master of your own life.

We become so involved in money affairs and see them as such a drag. They hold us back from doing this or that, getting this or that. By doing this, we are hoarding our past. Whatever little money we get, we hoard it. We are so afraid to let it flow. We do not realize that, when the two types of energy, positive and negative, are not in balance, the getting and giving are not in balance either. There is no mastery and no current. Money is a form of energy exchange that creates a current, a flow. It is an alternating current that goes up and down. Every time you think it is down, it may suddenly go up. Sometimes we are pleased it is up, but it may suddenly go down.

31

We have the capacity to keep energy flowing and to empower others with it. I love the word "empower." "E" equals Energy in motion with power. Do you see the difference between overpowering and empowering? When you encounter someone who stands over you and says, "I know it better!" you can smile and say, "Gee, you are trying to overpower me and intimidate me but I cannot be intimidated because I know." The knowing is a very important part. But knowing only comes through living it, experiencing it, and not avoiding it. When you see an obstacle, know that you are going to go beyond it, do not fight it.

Today, we still assume or believe that there are only two ways to deal with and master life. These two are, fight or flight, with no in-between way. The only time we have to fight or flee is when we have no mastery. The moment you have achieved mastery, there is neither fighting nor fleeing. Knowing and acting upon that knowing is the in-between way. The in-between way occurs when these two aspects integrate, moving forward, upward and beyond the obstacles.

As long as we, as a society, keep saying, "These are the two ways you can do it, either fight or flight," we deny the self's capacity. It is denying the statement, "Ye can do the things I do and greater things can ye do." You will start looking for greater things, but as long as you are going to flee, you will never know what you are fleeing from. If you are going to fight, you will destroy it. After you have destroyed it, you will not know what you destroyed because there is nothing to prove what it was anymore except havoc—a lack of harmony.

32

You have an inner knowing to activate, to radiate out, that puts powerful energy in motion in every situation. Think about David and Goliath. Often things which stand so gigantically in front of you are, in reality, phantoms. Phantoms of your mind. A denial of yourself. To be small and walk ten feet tall is the mastery of life. It is from the smallest seeds that jungles, forests, and orchards grow.

The Scriptures say, "If you just had the faith of a mustard seed, you could move mountains." Do not take this literally about mountains. Daily, you are surrounded by mountains of opposition. They are there to release the faith from the mustard seed. Your soul essence is already endowed with all the qualities of growth, all the qualities of fruition. It is only through mastery of life and self that we share the fruits of our beingness. It will then not be necessary to speak about freedom. You show that no matter what your surroundings, you are free to activate.

The freedom that we have been celebrating so much has been freedom from parents, school, employers, income tax, etc. Do you realize this falls into the category of flight? All your protests are not going to do anything unless you live your protest. Let your beingness be a protest. Act upon that protest. Carrying signs may be helpful, but, to some extent, is that not asking for confirmation from others that you are right? Do you need to advertise your wares? Exhibit your beingness.

Religion is the same. As long as you have to state, "I am this or I am that. . . . I follow this or that philosophy. . . ." it has no value. What you are asking is, "Do you agree with me?" Is this going to strengthen you? Are you not strong enough to stand up and say, "This is what I know. Therefore, I will live it, in spite of everything else."

Think of all these people around the world who now have freedom to exhibit their beliefs, their knowingness. That is the freedom we are acquiring. Not just a wall tumbling down but millions of walls falling down, walls within hearts, minds, and bodies. They go down brick by brick. Realize that this is the beginning of harmony and peace in the world. It is something happening within us. We are beginning to appreciate the freedom we have.

No one in this whole world can intimidate you in your knowingness and faith in your beingness. To me, that is expressing mastery of life. Go straight forward, walk through the walls, if there are still walls there. Do not fight or flee them. When we can see it that way, then we can say, "I recognize now that I am a master." You do not have to wait. Recognize that today. Do not flee from all the things that are happening in your body. It takes maintenance and sustenance of your body to attain mastery of life. They are all integral. This is a glorious thing to know. Today, together with you, I feel we are celebrating this mastery of life and new found freedom "for," instead of freedom "from."

DIVINITY

Rejoice, people, this is the time,

> *To realize your being, to become sublime.*

Throughout the world, the truth is revealed,

> *Through freedom of faith, the earth will be healed.*

Freedom for spirit, body, and mind,

> *Uniting the world and people of all kinds.*

The cause, the spirit, the fruit; this Trinity

> *Gave birth to all, assuring its true Divinity.*

Bringing peace on earth with bliss,

> *Oh, what a time for joy this is.*

With open heart and shining bright,

> *We give our pledge that in God we unite.*

6

YOUR UNKNOWN SELF

WHAT A JOYFUL TIME IT IS, INDEED! In 2 Cor. 6, I read something very contemporary with the world today. We are given the chance again to be free in our thoughts, speech, and living. We now are finding within ourselves the understanding that the unknown self is the God within; the divinity does speak, but we have not heard.

In Corinthians, God says,

I have listened to you in an acceptable time and I have helped you on the day of salvation. Behold! Now is the acceptable time. And, behold! Now is the day of salvation! Give no occasion for offense to anyone in anything so that there be no blemish in our ministry but, in all things, let us show ourselves to be the ministers of God in much patience, in tribulations, in receptivity, in necessities and in imprisonment, in scorchings, in bombs, in toilings, in vigils, in fastings, by purity, by knowledge, by long suffering, by kindness, by the Holy Spirit, by sincere love, by the word of truth, by the power of God, by the armor of righteousness on the right hand and on the left, by honor and dishonor, by praise and reproach. As unknown and yet well known, as dying and behold, we live, so chastened and not dying; as sorrowful, yet always rejoicing; as poor, yet enriching many; and, having nothing and yet possessing all things.

This is actually the message we see coming from our unknown self. The quest of our lives is to make that unknown known. The spark of divinity given to all of us is beginning to light a fire and shine over this world. Yes, they are only sparks at this moment. Maybe they are only simple words coming from our heart into our being. When we look in the eyes of those who suffer, we realize we have not always been united. Healing needs to take place from within. The healing coming from within you now supports those who are suffering. All those who have suffered will receive your light.

36   Now is the time for you to become a more radiant being because the darkness which has surrounded everyone in the world is ready to be lifted. Let your light shine from your unknown self and make it known to this world.

You are one of those who were born in this divinity. As we celebrate the birth of Christ, it is the appropriate time to understand that it is actually the birth of the light. This light is coming through the darkness. If we have ever been in a state where we needed self-healing, this is the time. By awakening self-healing, you will heal this world.

Now is the time to speak from within our hearts; not in words, but in rays of light that can shine upon everyone. Your unknown self needs to become the known self in every second of your life. Realize that you have been given the understanding of a divine being: everlasting power existing throughout eternity. We are the living light which God gave to this world, for each to do his or her work and, through us, to let God experience life as it is.

The unknown self is a beautiful state of being when we, in the silence of our own sanctuary, our heart, dive in and hear this silent voice. The silent voice constantly promises to maintain that faith and hope which we have always had, but not always used. Rejoice, the time is here not only to find this point of hope but to use it and bring it to those who are still lacking hope.

It says in the Scriptures that, "when we speak, our mind should be a whole mind." It should be the mind which speaks, and then our speech becomes prophecy. Grasping this prophecy, we make the unknown self the known self in our daily living.

Today is a special day, like every day is a special day. Every day a new state of healing takes place in all of us. It is by the light, by the god given Christ that we find in our beingness a better understanding of our function, duties, and rights. Our freedom of being is now awakening to us. We can bring it into practice now, more than ever before. I think if we can make this unknown self our daily task, we will be blessed, as we always were blessed. Now we will understand how blessed we are in this world.

37

VITALITY

The principle of life, "Vitality,"

    Expression of strength, the reality.

Love, the source of this great wealth,

    Vitality brings forth our spiritual health.

Whenever our physical strength is about to fail,

    Tis the power of spirit which surely prevails.

Compassion, love expressed with joy at heart,

    Gives the principle of Life its primal start.

From then on radiance gets its worth,

    To shine its rays and strengthen the earth.

Providing us, on life a new lease,

    To celebrate equality, freedom, and peace.

· 7 ·

DOMINION AND EMPOWERMENT

I T IS DIFFICULT TO FIND THE APPROPRIATE EXPRESSION FOR THE WORD "VITALITY." We use it often but do not realize what it really means. It is the principle of life. We must understand how we got it. In Genesis, it states that we were given the dominion of this earth.

Our dominion has not only its rights and benefits, it also has its duties. On 25 December, a new birth came forth, a "leader" or guide to make us aware and to remind us that we were put in dominion on this earth. Therefore, we have rights to gather the harvest from the work we do, provided for by the great creative force we call God. It is our duty to empower this force and to give it emotion to become a growing, constantly changing state of consciousness to a higher level.

Christmastime is a sign of new life, new vitality, as expressed by the light that came to shine upon us. A sign for us to become aware of a new level of consciousness. Remember, the star shone in the sky, guiding people to the new birth. It is not just by accident that we chose 25 December. It was a day in which the new idea came to light, of new life about to start.

The Christmas tree is a symbol of the tree of life with its greenness now adorned, with its symbols of goldlike suns in the sky. The angels on the tree announce the coming of a new beginning in which we, more than ever, need to realize that it is our duty to empower. It is the fulfillment of our own being to activate the life within. This vitality, this new life, gives us the capacity to bring peace, help, and healing to all.

Ps. 72 states it so clearly: "The mountains shall bring peace to the people and the little hills by righteousness. He shall judge the poor of the people; he shall save the children of the needy and shall break in pieces the oppressor." I think if we look around us, this is what is happening. We live not only with oppression brought about by some world leaders, but also with oppression by each other when we do not allow others to partake in this dominion.

40

We seemingly live in a field of freedom but in reality we are oppressed by the judgments of others. We attend this oppression. We play the game as much as everyone else. Now is the time to start saying, "Yes, we take dominion. We are going to take care, not only of this earth, but of everyone who exists on this earth." We are going to take care by bringing the healing power within ourselves to such a radiance that it will shine upon every part of this world. The healing takes place from within, where the radiance of the new light shines, giving rays of hope and action.

We can all, as individuals, bring the dominion of earth to an abundant harvest. Peace on earth will become a reality when no one is oppressed, even by their own feelings and knowingness. When we doubt our own function, we doubt our inner being, causing fear of change. We may not change in the manner in which we need to change. We may change by becoming diseased, by feeling a lack of being loved; *ill,* as in "*I Lack Love.*" When we allow ourselves to be oppressed, we suppress our inner feelings and do not express the love we feel burning inside. We must begin taking dominion of this earth by first taking dominion of ourselves.

If you look back through the ages, every time a new state occurs, an expansion of consciousness takes place. Then we become self-centered, we develop an idea of *how* things should be. We start to proclaim our oppression to the world, thereby sitting in judgment. Instead of the righteousness in which the Psalm speaks, it becomes a self-righteousness. A self-righteousness in which we do not express in totality all our functions. We see many people wanting to learn more about this consciousness and yet not portraying it in their daily life.

It is not just having knowledge of things. It is the knowingness that gives us our beingness. A knowingness that, no matter what happens to us, we hold to our principles of vitality, power, and force. We all have to forgive. Then this tree of life becomes the symbol that we give life continuously. By our radiance and power we bring it forth to empower others, rather than to overpower them. Overpowering has been taking place over the last several centuries.

I come from a country that has gone through occupation after occupation by oppressing forces. These forces have now become a lesser power. This is because some of us realized that we do not need to be oppressed. It is our duty to make sure that oppression does not happen again.

By maintaining our vitality, faith, and understanding of life, we do not need to survive for the sake of self, but for the sake of the rest of the world. We need to come out of this with a strengthened sense of power and spirit. It was thus that I decided, "This is my function. No matter what happens to me as a person, I have to go into this world to give dominion its right to fulfill within each person the capacity to set themselves free." Let us realize that when we take away the rights of dominion, we rob the earth of its wealth.

The Sufi, Hazrat Inayat Khan, says this in a beautiful way: "The worlds are held together by the heat of the sun. Each of us are atoms held in position by the eternal sun we call God." Within us is the same central power or vitality we call light. By the love of God we hold together the human spirit within our sphere or, lacking it, we let it fall.

Let us restore this dominion. Do not fail or fall but rise up en masse and give this world what it deserves: the empowerment of lasting peace from river to river, sea to sea, shore to shore, earth to sky, star to star, planet to planet, soul to soul. Then we will be able to sing, "Let there be peace on earth and let it begin with me!"

ANGEL

In the darkened sky, stars shining bright,

    Angels prepare to bring us light.

Announcing the birth of peace and love,

    Filling our hearts with faith from above.

To let us know, angels we too will be,

    Beaming, shining, radiant, for all to see.

Trumpets sounding within our soul,

    Giving us faith in becoming whole.

The message "awaken to truth," let ignorance fall;

    By shining our light we respond to the call.

Breathing the spirit of life anew,

    Angelic happiness for all, not just the few.

Rejoice now, you angels to be,

    Let peace on earth be our spiritual decree.

EVERYTHING IS POSSIBLE

THIS IS A SPECIAL DAY, AS IS EVERY DAY. Throughout the ages, 25 December has been a day of bringing forth new ideas and light, which brings us to a greater consciousness. We are all shepherds. Everything is possible, for every day is the birthday of new life from which we died out of the old state of consciousness.

Even though we may not be totally at peace within our own hearts and souls, we are reminded to give. The presents we give are actually fruits of our labor. No matter how big or small these gifts, your giving shows the thought and feeling of sharing the fruits of your labor. The greatest fruits are, of course, that you become conscious of all the things you succeeded and failed at.

Before we go into this new life, we need to see that we are still not totally at peace within ourselves. We need to direct ourselves to bring gifts to those with whom we are not totally at peace. Everything is possible if we see that this day is still celebrated with the same purpose, to announce the coming of a new level of consciousness: the Christ consciousness.

In practically every religion, even in pagan times, there was the celebration of the God, the Sun, bringing new light with which to grow an abundance of the fruits of work. This brings us to the understanding that toiling is not just for gain in the material sense. Everything we do with feeling brings out our potentials; thus, nothing is impossible. The limits are of our own making; we perceive them as limits. Even though we may not agree with another, or be "one" in our thoughts and our hearts, we are still "one." Recognize this.

We have seen "spontaneous remissions" take place. We were told, "These people no longer have any possibility of survival in the physical world." But still, they did survive. The love struck them and they realized that their time had not yet come. There was still a lot to do, even if it was just to become a shepherd to say, "Look! I was down but I am coming up to show you that anything is possible." It can happen if it is done in your higher state of consciousness, where logic can put aside the entrancing ideas of outside authorities. It is the inner voice which says, "I myself can do it."

The last couple of years have seen interesting developments in our world. No one thought it was possible to open the borders between the two Germanys. No one thought it was possible to open the Brandenburg Gate. No one thought it was possible that in a day's time people would wake up en masse and speak out against oppressors. Everything is possible. In all these years not only were they oppressed, but we were oppressed, too. We had abundance and took it for granted. We oppressed ourselves, our own beingness, by not sharing what we had to give.

We are becoming aware that we have been living in a world of greed. The 1980s were a decade of greed. We were shepherded in the wrong direction, obsessed by the twinkle of false gold. The gold which really has value is right within you; it is the wisdom that nothing in the universe is impossible because it follows the law. It is only we who are against the law, who are not fulfilling the law.

The only way we will discover self is by discovering ourselves within others, seeing the reflection of our own actions within others. This Christmas day is a day in which we can joyfully but solemnly start looking for that light which shines upon the dark crevices within ourselves. Awaken to that and recognize that the light is still there and that by fulfilling our function, nothing is impossible.

Many times during our travels it seemed there were impossibilities confronting us, but when we look back we recognize that these impossibilities just disappeared and things became possible again. Why? We discovered that by having faith and knowingness, we could bring new ideas and thoughts into fulfillment. The guiding light is there, even in the fog, if we are willing to share our being and become shepherds who were never lost. Even in an icy state, we can still feel that we can shine through and defrost our hearts. The frost is only a cover-up of the warmth we have for each other. When traveling we sometimes are embarrassed to show this. It is fascinating to see people really embrace each other. They do not hesitate to touch, not only with their beingness, but also physically, and say, "Wow! It is good to see you. It is nice to be with you." It is nice to have the light shine upon you as a sharing process takes place.

The message that everything is possible must be ingrained within us daily, not only at Christmastime. Every day that we confront ourselves and say, "That is impossible!" we negate our own capacities. With effort, everything is possible. We have also forgotten that we are endowed with all these potentials and capabilities. We must bring our worthiness to a higher state. Recognize that we are already angels, in the sense of being light-bringers. Do not hide your light under a bush any longer. Now is the time to shine out and make the things that seemed impossible, possible.

Celebrate this time as a growth state: the opening of the flower of faith and the birth of a new life. Even though we may be decrepit, poor in the material sense, or our body not functioning well anymore, new vitality can come in because everything is possible. Remember how it comes about. The time of taking things for granted has ended. Every little improvement within ourselves benefits everyone in the universe. Therefore, we do not need to look back, but rather, look forward recognizing what we can add.

Can you imagine the legacy you will leave behind from what has happened in this decade? How we have broken out from our imprisonment of consciousness! We needed to be driven to that point. We had become lackadaisical. We had not recognized the suffering around us. As long as we had what we had, that was okay. Now is the time for true sharing to begin, particularly the sharing of our beingness. Through our beingness it is possible to see the ray of light and fulfill our capacity to bring a new state of consciousness into the world. Everything is possible!

COMMITMENT

It seems, from the start to the end,

　　That the way we must travel is crooked and bent.

Though we often will go astray,

　　It is our commitment which shows the way.

Entrusted with a function, a charge to fulfill,

　　We keep on walking and direct our will.

To create a better world for all to be

　　Healthy, harmonious, and free.

· 9 ·

OVERCOMING OBSTACLES

W HEN WE TALK ABOUT COMMITMENT TO OUR FUNCTION IN LIFE, WE ENCOUNTER MANY DIFFERENT OBSTACLES. Actually, obstacles provide us with opportunities to challenge life. Overcome the obstacles and you perceive what lies beyond them. We need to be committed to our growth pattern to fulfill our own individual function. It is so beautiful that everyone on earth comes with a specific function and the perfect tool kit.

When we are born, we create an environment that gives us the opportunities to see these obstacles. This brings us a new understanding of what our function may be. Often, our greatest commitment lies in the state of beholding innocence, the innocence of our life. Recognize what obstacles hold us back from this innocent state. When it says in the Scriptures, "Let them become like children," this is actually saying, we came as children and we need to go as children, using humor and wit spontaneously from our heart.

We have the ability to overcome obstacles. Our emotions need to be expressed, no matter what. Our greatest obstacles are the stagnations caused by our perceptions of the outer world. We do not always recognize that every obstacle which comes our way is a challenge, a challenge to overcome and gain insight into our knowingness. We must constantly go within ourselves and find one point by which we can take the next step.

Start looking at what your obstacles are. Most obstacles are leftover emotions we have not dealt with; parts we did not feel we had the capacity to deal with. We forgot we had the tools to overcome these obstacles.

Disease is one aspect, a complex aspect, of not overcoming obstacles. Disease is a stagnation of energy within our body that we did not allow to come forth, we did not express it. This results in us becoming aware of the pressures around us. We are not always able to grab within ourselves the power to set our energy free to move through the obstacle. Do not go around or avoid the obstacles. Innocently and truthfully walk forward and deal with it.

48

Each obstacle we have, such as spite, jealousy, envy, hate, or blindness to what is happening within others, occurs when we have no awareness of what is happening within ourselves. Do not sit in judgment of what others put in front of us.

Obstacles are things we have not faced within ourselves. We become disturbed and perturbed with the fact that they seem to be the cause of what holds us back from total expression. Look deep within yourself. When we only feel envy or jealousy in others, we are unable to see we have similar abilities. We also have gifts that they are envious of.

In reality, we have not recognized our own stagnant inner self. We do not express our capacity to deal with our outer environment when we have not dealt with our inner environment. There is no way our outer environment can be treated any differently than our inner self. When we have self-doubt, when we feel less endowed by the Creator, we go out and try to establish a state in which we are not faithful or truthful to ourselves.

The obstacle of pride is another aspect that holds us back. We do not dare bring out and act upon that challenge. The opposite of this occurs when we do good deeds and then immediately fill ourselves with pride. This demolishes the original good deed. We are advertising how great we are, rather than saying, "All right, I did that because it was my commitment to life." We should not be satisfied with it and certainly not let our hearts fill with pride, for "I have been such a good being." This is difficult.

I am reminded of the story of a master's pupil who was sent into the desert charged with and committed to fasting. He had to fast for a certain length of time. As he walked in the desert with two hours still to go on his fast, be became very thirsty. He got so thirsty he could hardly wait to reach an oasis and drink. Finally he arrived at one with a beautiful artesian well. He still had an hour and a half of fasting to go, according to his master's charge and his commitment. He was so thirsty he bent over to drink and, just as the drops of water were going to touch his lips, he remembered his fast and stopped himself. As he walked away, his heart filled with pride that he had overcome his thirst and was still following the fast. The moment he noted that his heart filled with pride, he ran back to the spring and drank. "It is better to break a rule than to let your heart fill with pride."

This story has always struck me. I, too, find myself feeling this self-satisfaction and pride when I have done something. Not realizing that at that moment, I stagnate what I tried to accomplish. I also block others because they cannot relate to my real self or resonate with my inner being when I am filled with pride.

Often, in my seminars I state that I am a very dissatisfied, content person. It sounds like a paradox! But, to me, that is the only way to overcome the obstacles of pride, envy, jealousy, and what have you. What do I mean when I say this? I mean I am dissatisfied with everything I do and I am also very content with what I do, but the next time it will not be okay. This prevents my heart from filling with pride.

However, most people are dissatisfied. I am not so special by being dissatisfied with everything I do. But, the moment most people are dissatisfied, they go to the wailing wall and find reasons and excuses as to why they are dissatisfied. If their father or mother or whoever had not done this or that to them when they were three years old, they would be better people now. Or, if it were not for that neighbor who did this or that, they would have done it better.

The wailing wall always surrounds us, even though the walls are now coming down. Maybe we have not yet dealt with the wall. Our wailing wall is still there whenever we use reasons and excuses why we did not do as well as we should or could have done.

Well, I am dissatisfied, all right. But at the same time I ask myself the questions, "Who made me do it this way?" I did. "Why have I still not done it correctly? Why have I not overcome that obstacle?" Then I ask myself, "Did I do the best I could for now?" Yes, I did. Therefore, I am content, filled with joy that I did the best I could. At the same time recognizing it is not yet the best.

50

Even in the Scriptures it says, "The best is yet to be." Luckily, we do not know exactly what the best is. The best for now is not good enough for two seconds from now. This is, again, a challenge to overcome obstacles. The greatest obstacles we encounter are the ones that we look for some cause from the past, rather than looking for challenges in the future.

We need faith in ourselves, that we did the best we could at that time with the tools we had. Tools we may not even have known we had and we may have been surprised when they came to the surface. The challenge to overcome gives you the power to fulfill your commitment to life.

When you fulfill your commitment to life, you automatically commit it to everyone in your environment. You will not compare if you did it better or lesser than someone else. You will know that you are comparing your best for now with the best you just finished. You recognize that you took a step on your path of knowing, the path of consciousness, the fulfillment of your commitment.

It is a joyful state when we recognize that we have fulfilled part of our commitment and that we are still on our way. When we understand that, then we can say, "If you have as much faith as a mustard seed, you can move mountains."

You must not "pooh pooh" away every little thing you do because it was not big enough. Everything starts from a seed. It is the growing and evolving from a seed that will eventually give you fruit. Recognize that when it says in the Scriptures, "By their fruit will ye know them," it is not by advertising how great you were or what you have or have not done that you will be known. Your "fruit" comes from your actions. Let your actions show that you are overcoming your obstacles.

What will your fruit be? Your fruit will be that you are happier and healthier, because you are expressing things that make you whole. As long as we do not express ourselves in totality with knowingness, we are not whole. We must move toward wholeness in order to maintain this state of commitment to life.

Do not look if another person's function is different. "Vive la difference!" Be glad we are all different so we can look at and share our differences with each other, instead of comparing our differences and sitting in judgment about which are better, good or bad.

Overcome the idea that we need to be "good." Most people do not have a proper understanding of what good really means. The Creator gave us everything when he created the heavens, earth, and everything on it and called it "good." How can you, then, be anything else but good? It is your own blindness to this innate, inner goodness that makes you call yourself bad.

If you constantly feel you do not have the power to overcome your obstacles, then you will feel that you cannot handle every little obstacle. You then regress into your past rather than progress to your future. It is you who make your future. The more obstacles you overcome, the brighter the future will be for you.

Recognize that the energy all of us are made of, constantly needs to be active and creative. Every act we do is not just acting "as if," it is acting out because "it is." Do not playact, acting as if it is not a reality. Every obstacle can become a reality; every overcoming can become a reality. In this way you are able to expand yourself into full consciousness and you have done your best for that moment, thereby following your commitment to your life. This is not just for yourself but also for your environment. It benefits from your capacity to overcome these obstacles. This is very important.

I will say again and repeat to you, "Whatever happens to you, happens to the whole ocean." It is like what Paramahansa Yogananda said: "You are a drop in the ocean. Whatever happens to the drop happens to the whole ocean. Whatever happens to the ocean happens to every drop." Through your beingness you cannot fail to affect others.

With every ray of light, let go, shine out, and direct it upon your obstacles and it will shine through them. You are the healers of this world. You are given and shown challenges through obstacles. By your radiance, you help others to become more radiant. You are the starters of fires, the inspiration for other people. We do not need to go out, we can sit silently, radiate out, and overcome the obstacles. It is like a laser beam. The more powerful your radiance becomes, the brighter the world will shine and the less shadows there will be.

We must always remember to face the light whenever we walk the path of life. Face the light so that the shadow falls behind you. The moment you turn your back on the light, your shadow is in front of you. That is a well-known scientific fact. In the Scriptures it says: "Satan, get thee behind me." Satan is, of course, those shadows you sometimes try to follow.

When you do not see the light any longer, you know you are not shining enough. Your own shadow becomes darker and darker. Just turn around. Face the light and you will see the shadow behind you. These shadows are the obstacles of life. When you go through them and deal with them, your own light shines and resonates.

This sounds very philosophical. The best proof is when you become healthier. You can say, "I have overcome those little stagnations that held me back from the total fulfillment of my being." So, wherever you go, shine your light and overcome your obstacles, thereby overcoming the obstacles that are now facing us in the world.

AWE

In awe, I stand in the foothills of the majestic mountain,

    Overwhelmed by thoughts of the mind's all-knowing fountain.

To behold what the Creator with nature has wrought,

    Fills me with respectful thought.

To know that I, too, in this creation's play,

    Have a part, every night and every day.

In the stillness of the human heart, I will be,

    For always, filled with awe, I will see.

54

Regina Marga

· 10 ·

EXPANDING CONSCIOUSNESS

AVE YOU FELT THE EXPANSION OF CONSCIOUSNESS THAT IS TAKING PLACE ALL THE TIME? Whenever you go into meditation, start feeling change within you. You will begin to experience things about which you may only have had knowledge of.

First, grasp what consciousness is. It is a quality of the energy that we are made of. We must understand that consciousness cannot expand unless the energy, which is qualitative, also expands. It is an active state of being.

Even in our meditations when we seem to be in the silence, in reality we are awakening a lot of activity within us. This activity has the capacity to break down things which stagnated us. These things are a product of what we have *knowledge* of rather than what we know them to mean to us as individual beings.

When you expand your consciousness, the first expansion takes place within you. Thereby you affect your outer environment. Expanding consciousness just for the "I" self only sweeps dust under the rug. We do not see it any longer, so we may feel changed. In everyday life when you kick the rug, dust clouds come up again. We need to realize that expansion of consciousness is not a state of ignorance but an opposite state. By removing ignorance from the shelves piled up in front of your eyes, you can see your own truth and how it relates to your expression in the world.

Expansion of consciousness is a continuous activation of the flow of the energy we are made of, an exciting state. When thoughts come to the surface, we get the feeling of knowing. We already know and now we feel it within our own physical being.

Quite often during the day, someone makes a statement and you are not sure if their words are the truth. You will feel it. You get this, "Uh huh, I know that. I feel this. I experience this." Grasp that truth, activate it, and express it creatively in your activities.

56

So often we misunderstand creativity. It is not just making something look different that is, in reality, just old refurbished stuff. Rather, it is creating a new activity or state of being. We often fool ourselves and feel highly creative, but lack the feeling of excitement in doing it. The excitement needs to become so strong that it becomes a state of ecstasy, contained ecstasy.

Speaking in scientific terms, we say we need to increase the amplitude of our brain waves to have greater insight and intuition. This amplitude comes from within. The word "amplitude" means to amplify, to put power behind something. The power increases do not just happen in the brain or by just turning on a switch or pressing a button. Through our total activity, the total physical body, this power is a vibration from our toes to our hair. This state of internal excitement breaks down stagnant chemistry, activating molecules and setting free enhanced atoms which were imprisoned in these molecules.

When we say, "It matters not," it means taking energy out of its material form and setting it free to form new ideas, activities, and a new state of beingness. That state of ecstasy comes from within and is part of our total being. Being in ecstasy causes physical changes to take place. The atoms become electrically charged—positive, negative, and neutral—and function as catalysts to bring wholeness.

The aspect of healing depends upon our capacity to expand our consciousness. When we perceive consciousness as a quality of energy and expand it, the energy surrounding us also expands, not just the energy within our body. The body lets go and sets energy free. We can then resonate with the higher levels of knowingness. We can say we are becoming "in tune with." We become intuitive. It is not just getting flashes; it is a continuous state of being in touch with the divine nature of the universe, the all-knowing state, universal truth, it is taking that truth and acting upon it.

Expanded consciousness is a state of much more love than what we claim as love, such as when we do good for someone else or for ourselves for approval's sake. Although this is an aspect of love, it is not its totality. The totality of love is maintaining a state of expanded consciousness for forty-eight hours a day; always keeping it in mind and body, acting on it continuously. In setting this energy free, recognize its creative aspects in the outer world and how we touch and stimulate others to action.

57

When we say we need to become inspirational, understand that "inspire" means "to set on fire." Without fire and activity, there is no life. When we perceive the universe during the night as a very dark environment, we forget that this darkness is filled with light. Nothing will happen unless we inspire or activate it. Even with darkness in your life, there is only one way to see the light again: by inspiring yourself. When breathing, instead of saying "inhaling," say, "Inspiring. I inspire. With every breath I activate the electricity which sets the photons in the darkness of my own soul and body free."

With every breath we take, we must recognize where it comes from. This breath does not come from within but from without and becomes the within. We need to center the without at the source of light and activate it there, so we can inspire and set our light free.

Whenever we start activating this light, there is always a crisis before the healing. We like to avoid that and have the light always there. The crisis that takes place when healing occurs, awakens us to the truth and sets in motion a process which has order, even though it feels chaotic within us. It is a state of entropy. We need to activate it, not hold on to it.

When we try to avoid the crisis symptoms, we stagnate our wholeness, our own healing process. Recognize that when we amplify, we also amplify the symptoms through the changes which occur within us. That is part of the expansion of our consciousness. We begin seeing the symptoms clearly for what they are. Take these symptoms and say, "Hallelujah! Things are becoming clearer to me. Now I know I have to make changes. I cannot just stop the symptoms to avoid changes."

Nothing that happens in your life, no matter how great the future may look, happens without some struggle. The struggle is part of continuously getting into the state of ecstasy. Ecstasy comes from within and sets the light free. The struggle maintains the ecstatic state. It continuously amplifies it so that we radiate beautiful waves of light from our whole body which then resonate with the universal truth, giving us insight. The more insight we get, the clearer our sight.

By setting our light free, every step we physically take on earth allows an exchange of radiance to take place. The more ecstatic you are, the more amplified your energy is. The more expanded your consciousness is, the more you treat the earth with greater respect, in a state of "awe." A sharing then takes place with the earth and with everything that lives on it.

Let me tell you the story about a lady who had to leave and, during her absence, asked someone to care for her home for a couple of months. Before she left, she asked the person to take good care of her roses. Well, the person was very busy and did not pay much attention to the roses. She took care of the house but not the roses. When the lady returned, the roses were nearly dead.

The lady stood in front of the rose bushes and radiated her love for the roses. She was sad, but she knew she had to overcome her sadness in order to give life to her plants. She needed to use that sadness to be more determined that these roses could return to life. She began talking to the roses and standing in awe about this beautiful aspect of nature. Within a couple of days the roses started to come to life again and bloom beautifully.

We have human roses all around us. They too have thorns, and sometimes it is hard to stand in awe of their being. When we say we need to respect each other, we do not mean respect because of status, degree, or financial capacity, but respect because they are part of nature. We need to have a feeling of awe, for everything is capable of changing. We need to be in awe of our own capacities to expand our consciousness and enhance whoever comes into our environment.

Then we can really celebrate Valentine's Day every day, exchanging that ecstatic state of expansion of consciousness from our heart to their heart. We do not need words for that. I do not think the lady stood and actually spoke to the roses, but she connected with them from within herself. She radiated whatever was needed. If we can do this with our roses of human nature, we will see them bloom, too.

59

A fascinating aspect of roses is that the more you cut them, the more that come forth. We treat them with respect and awe by putting them in our environment and feeling their velvety softness. This overcomes the sting of the thorn. We are not only healing self but are fully involved in the evolution of the whole world and whoever lives there. That is the purpose of expanding our consciousness.

You came here into this world at this particular time. Every day, when I hear the news, I stand in awe that we are finally starting to get there. We are beginning to recognize that we all have the right to freedom "for." There is an equality within each of us making us beautiful and radiant. A spark of joy coming in.

We now see how we have suppressed, oppressed, and repressed our inner feelings for so many decades. We have not shared our real being; we just act as if we had. We had all kinds of excuses why we could not find equality. Now the universe is practically driving us into that state. There is hardly any capacity to resist it any longer. It makes us, as individuals, feel an inner urge to participate.

We have spent so much time living this life to be free from this or that. Now there is an inner, worldwide feeling that there is freedom for the good of all. If we can expand our consciousness to that state and qualify ourselves to have a higher capacity of living, we will indeed have a Valentine's Day, night, hour, minute, and second in every part of our lives. That is my wish for you and for myself.

FREEDOM

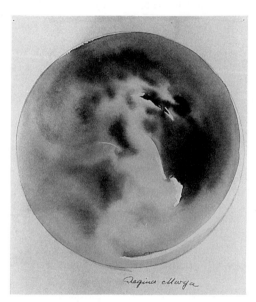

The urge in all people is to be free,

From all kinds of oppression and tyranny.

Freedom is a necessity to become whole,

To attain full expression of body, mind, and soul.

Searching within to find truth that sets us free,

Following a path of knowing and love, so it will be.

All will celebrate freedom's call with victory!

· 11 ·

SUPREMACY VERSUS SUPERIORITY

61

SUPREMACY AND SUPERIORITY ARE TWO ASPECTS THAT SEEM TO BE SIMILAR IN NORMAL, DAILY LIVING. The antagonistic state of superiority actually enhances imprisonment, not freedom. When we feel superior, we are not looking at the higher state of our being. We have assumed that we have reached the higher state of our being and therefore have superiority over others. This is an imprisonment of other people's freedom to discover their own capacities and abilities. It does not allow them to enlighten themselves and become active within the society.

We have used the word "supremacy" in a totally opposite way to its real meaning. Supremacy means the highest, best, or greatest. Superiority is expressed only through one's own personal will and is based predominantly upon assumed knowledge—knowledge assumed to be the highest, best, or greatest. In reality, it only means that it is higher than the former, never the highest. Even a person who does not have much knowledge can still act as a superior being over and upon someone with less knowledge. As a result, we are constantly in conflict with our own inner freedom.

In his book, *I and Thou*, Martin Buber makes it very clear that the "I" is never supreme, but the "I" can be superior based upon what it has perceived from the supreme. It still has to move on to a higher state of being in order to achieve the supreme. Can we achieve the supreme? In my opinion, we cannot. We cannot achieve the highest, best, and greatest because we can not become what we already are. We can only attain awareness of it. The awareness will be blocked from us if we act on the "I" ego and feel superior. This action blinds us from what we are already. It actually stops us from learning to know. Knowingness comes from experiencing our experiences. It does not come from interpreting our experiences. Experiencing is just one of the steps toward knowing the supreme.

In this life, we cannot assume we will have total understanding of the universal creative force which we call the supreme. We hear people saying, "I am God," but not living it. They are just verbalizing it, which creates a lot of antagonism. They proclaim themselves to be supreme and do not understand that that is a statement of superiority, a judgment. Therefore, we are in continuous conflict. No wonder we see protests. They will not give us the freedom to be.

Whenever we label something, we start identifying with it. We then can feel we are better than others as we are already on the path and the others have not yet discovered it. Though they follow a path similar to ours, it will never be the same. They may not label it the same. This will hold us back from the freedom to be.

In Hindu philosophy, they also talk about the supreme being. In the Vedanta, a difference is made between the soul and the spirit. The soul is the essence of this supreme aspect and the spirit keeps the soul in action. The soul constantly reminds us that we have not yet achieved total awareness of this universal aspect. Hindus do not say, "I am God." They say, "God am I." They surrender to the higher knowingness of being.

The more we work on understanding "God am I," the more we will start to live and express it. We will stop sitting in judgment of those whom we assume have not recognized the fact of the "God am I" state. This lack of understanding, this type of judgment, holds us back. This new era will only be new when we live it in a new way.

In the "I" self, the superior self, there is a past. We base our actions of today upon the past. In the supreme aspect there is no past. Alan Watts wrote a fantastic book called,

The Supreme Identity. He talks about the identity of the "I" and "Thou." Realize that everything we do by the "I" decision, does not listen to and perceive what the "Thou" gives us.

Our expression needs to come from the heart in a spontaneous way. When we spontaneously do this, we are not going to look at how someone else responds. If our response comes strongly from our heart, we know their response also comes from the heart. We may not conceptually be able to perceive this, but we create a resonant state with them by which words are no longer a means to understanding. Whenever we approach someone, we must never feel superior. We must remind ourselves that there is a supremacy or higher state within each of us.

The word "understanding" has a totally different meaning. It is a resonating and exchanging state of feeling, an experiencing of each other where you do not question the other's ability to follow up on what you suggest or advise them to do. It does not come from your superiority, but from your urge to be of service to them. That understanding becomes a matter of standing under the aspect of the supreme being, the surrender of superiority.

In our society there are courts, the highest court being the Supreme Court. It is still expression on a human level, but judgment is made rather than understanding. This is where we need to start looking. Conceptually, we constantly observe others, thereby avoiding the observation of ourselves. Only by self-observance will we know that we are never superior to anyone. We always have a relationship with their supremacy, with their supreme being and identity.

In some Christian philosophies, people greet each other with, "The Christ in you loves the Christ in me." This is recognition of the Christos—"The light within you loves the light within me"—a recognition of the supreme aspect. We must realize that every action from us needs to be based upon this recognition and it must come from a loving heart, not from a thinking mind. The thinking mind constantly questions others and rarely questions the self because of its assumption of superiority rather than recognizing the supreme aspect within.

In every meeting we need to bring out what the higher self dictates. The higher self dictates in a very gentle way while the dictation of the superior one is always a binding one, requiring us to abide by and be obedient to it. Even at this particular moment I am not teaching you obedience to what I say. As a matter of fact, I ask you to become disobedient to me or to whomever is in your environment. Be disobedient to them and become obedient to your inner knowing, feeling self.

64

Discovering that truth sets you free. Only when you are free will you allow others to be free. The moment you feel imprisoned, you also hold others back from their freedom. You may declare that you find something to be the truth, yet do not recognize that truth is not a constant state as you experience it. What you find to be your truth today will change tomorrow, because life is a continuous movement of evolution. Evolution means that we are "voluting" the energy. We are getting to know more through experiencing and through having the freedom to experience, whether in solitude, a crowd, or a marketplace.

Bring out your truth. That can never become a superior aspect because the moment you bring it out, it is in a state of change. When we drop the fear of "our" change, we will have the freedom to recognize supreme versus superior.

THE FUTURE

From the glory and downfall of the past,
    Shall it be that the future will be cast?
Acting upon all we have learned,
    Utilizing all we gained, all we earned.
Steadfastly forward, we begin to know,
    We always reap that which we sow.

The past, the present, and that which will be,
    Depends on my knowing that which I see.
Expanding my awareness in all I do,
    Will form my life and future, too.
By opening my heart to all life's needs,
    My future will be secured in spirit and deed.

· 12 ·

1991 VISIONS

HIS IS, INDEED, THE BEGINNING OF A NEW YEAR. All of you have become aware of it in one way or another. We have cast a certain mold that will determine what we are going to do and how the future will come forth.

The lotus is a perfect symbol for today. It is not for nothing that the Tibetan monks begin their meditations with, "Oh, beautiful lotus! Oh, beautiful jewel in the lotus! O mani pahdmi om." They repeat this over and over again to make themselves aware of the jewel in the lotus. Few of us have recognized the beauty of this flower, its purple colors of integration, because it grows from a decaying bulb down in the mud, and then, through its activity, recreates a new life symbol. The water from which the stem rises is the emotional plane, the energy in motion. It creates a new level of being. It is supported by its leaves, nicely resting on top of the water, steady upon the emotions. Then, there are the petals from which the bud slowly starts to open to show the beauty within.

Now, why is this such a good symbol for today? People are living upon a bulb called planet earth which is in a state of decay. Only through this decay is our future secure, for it shows that we need to become activated to realize what our future can and should bring. It has given us new opportunities from all the things we cast and molded in the past. We now have a chance to restore the earth and bring to it a new aspect.

We are starting to protest against what is happening to our environment, to the decaying bulb and the powers which appear to have taken over. We become indignantly affected by it and say this is not the way it should be. We need, now, to start finding the power within ourselves not to fight or protest, but rather to look at the future vision of a peaceful world. When you want to protest, you need to transform that issue into what you desire it to become. It is your identifying motive from which to work.

68

You are not really protesting against anything, just as you do not protest against diseases. Diseases are part of your transformation, but you keep identifying with them. You say you are working against them, trying to heal yourself. In reality, you are making yourself more suitable for these diseases to fester. You give them power by continuously calling on them, seemingly in order to fight them. You admit you are having a fight with them.

Start to perceive the opposite state. Do not protest against war, but rather protest for peace. We do not need to mention things that are not operating in their proper place.

Our future is going to depend on a very different economy. We have been an indulgent society. You possess potentials you have never used. Because of what cannot be done to and for you, you will be forced to find the potentials, strengths, and abilities within you that you have rarely activated. This year, in particular, is going to be a year of tremendous surprises. It will force us to act. Though it looks very dark, within the darkness is absorption of light which can only be activated **IF** you get involved.

There is no way in this new year we can evolve, unless we get involved. First, get involved within yourself. Set straight all that has not been harmonious within you. By doing that, you will support the whole world in its effort to achieve a state of harmony and peace.

Yes, we need to look at a different economy. Time is going so fast. We have to know the demands of what will be needed in the next year, so we can prepare ourselves for it. We cannot do this by haphazardly living. This is the time! This is really a glorious time we are given! We are practically forced to challenge and look within ourselves to find the potentials that will bring the future to a fantastic state. I see it as a very glorious state.

I know there will be more pain, but the more pain we have, the more glory we will attain when we have conquered that which seemed to be acting against us. This will not be achieved by fighting, but by learning to cooperate, and not cooperating as a mass, but as individuals. The mass can only function in a cooperative way. This means not all of us doing the same thing, but instead, each doing his or her own thing in the best way possible and cooperating through our contributions.

69

Competition will also fade out, one of the factors that caused our situation. When we continuously compete and compare, life becomes a contest rather than a flow of growth, maturity, and truth. This year can give you the opportunity to go straight forward, if you are willing not to back out from the dark clouds. Yes, there will be confusion, but it will redirect you.

It may seem that, many times in your life, you have been lost in certain situations. But there were always signs giving you direction, if you just looked for them within. The signs you saw were put there by others who thought it would be better for you to go this way or that. Quite often, you did not follow your path because the sign said, "You must be lost." In reality, you were on a new path to your own discoveries. When you followed the signs on the road, you found only what others had prepared for you, assuming they knew what you needed. Your own needs were never fulfilled. They did this, perhaps, with the best of intentions, but, because of them, we failed to perceive what our own path needed to be.

We are unique beings. At this time we have a chance to discover self, our true power within. We can empower ourselves and the whole world. This is our opportunity. The Aquarian Age is a totally different level of consciousness from any we have ever experienced. We were neither adapted to it nor totally prepared for it. Circumstances are forcing us to prepare for all situations.

You need to diversify and to live with diversity. Special groups will not stand out as better than others. It is ridiculous to talk of third worlds and their needs. There is only one world! We are part of the human family; brothers and sisters who all have equality. We need to discover that within ourselves. This may be why world circumstances are occurring at this time.

If ever there were a time to overcome your belief system by discovering your knowing system, this is the time. When everything moves smoothly, you can get whatever you need or think you need. In most cases, you did not need it in the first place.

We are going toward a state of austerity. This does not mean that we will deny our primal needs. We need to be more careful because things will be harder to get. We will have a much greater appreciation for what we receive.

Our future is based upon our past. We need to finish with the past. We have unfinished work ahead of us. In my vision, we will be more capable of celebrating every day, no longer taking our potentials for granted. Instead, we will utilize them more appropriately by becoming self-sufficient and not dependent.

We have seen our health system start to fail because most could not afford it. That, too, I see as a good sign because it drives us to discover, "Wow! I can do it myself!" I am not just talking about "self-help" methods. I have found that I can possess all the tools, molds, and techniques, but if I cannot put my heart into it, no tools will be helpful. We seem to go out everywhere to get tools.

This is the year we need to become willing. This is happening because circumstances are driving us toward it. Start utilizing and practicing these tools. Practice not only when something goes wrong, but to maintain your health status which now is more important than ever.

When you shine your light, no matter how dark it gets around you, even if you can only see a couple of feet ahead of you, world harmony will happen. Maybe there are some of us who see the future this way now and think, "I forgot to take my sunglasses off, it is so dark around me." No, it *is* that dark. You can make it light again, if you shine out, bring yourself to full capacity and put your heart into it. This means your inner systems will function in a cooperative way. Then I think the future will bring results which we cannot, at this moment, foresee because of the darkness.

I know that, inwardly, we are all at a level of hope where we can individually partake in the whole process. Therefore, this year, 1992, is going to be important for all of us as we create a greater state of health and wholeness. When we utilize outside sources, we need to be in tune with their direction with our hearts. Do not go out there and seek help for what you have the capacity to do yourselves.

You might need some assistance to confirm that you are on the right track. That is why we need to relate to each other and exchange and share with each other. We need to start expressing what is in our hearts, not what is in the cortex of our brains. We have to be honest, not only with each other, but particularly with ourselves.

Do you realize what is happening this year? We are removing the veils: the veils of ignorance, arrogance, and false status. I have walked this path a long time and do not yet see the end of it!

INTEGRITY

This is the start of a new decade in time,

    Another chance to attain the sublime.

At the final end of the decade of greed,

    We saw many from tyranny freed.

The redemption of liberty,

    Brought with it the need for integrity.

Acknowledging the state of our acquired grace,

    Proclaiming equality for the entire human race.

Together, making whole the earth,

    We'll assure this new decade its worth.

· 13 ·

Too Good To Be True

THE ASPECT OF INTEGRITY IS A VERY IMPORTANT PART OF OUR LIVES. We are quite willing to give up many things and often give up our integrity to fulfill so-called "personal needs." We forget that our personal needs may be in conflict with the needs of all. We all sometimes personally feel that we are the ones who are "deserving"; but if we understood this word, we would realize that what we think we deserve becomes a disservice to others. Therefore, we are not dealing with the state of integrity and begin to think things are "too good to be true."

In many ways, we grasp our expectations and forget about the state of integrity, not realizing these may not be glowing or functioning as well as they might. We get entranced by what we set out to achieve or attain and put everything else aside, thereby losing sight of the needs of the environment.

Any time we can place the word "too" in front of a statement, we are already losing the state of integrity. Integrity is the result of a process. It is the result of integration, harmonization, and balance. The moment balance is achieved, we must let go; otherwise, we become static.

Sometimes, with the idea that things are so good, we become less caring and observing of further needs. We are satisfied with what we have done. Satisfaction can become a dangerous aspect in that we quickly lose our balance. We wonder where does our level of integrity lie, beyond our logical opinions. Trying to make up our minds, we see a division occurring within our environment, suggesting an imbalanced state.

Many protests are happening now. I am for these protests. However, I think we must express what we really feel. How do we bring it out? I see and hear bitterness and lack of understanding. I still hear a striving for our own good and, consequently, a lack of recognition of what is good for others. These statements seem to mean the same thing: "I have a half full glass of water," or, "I have a half empty glass of water." The amount of water seems to be the same, but what am I looking for? What is my need? I must recognize what my needs are while I look at my opinions.

So, are we going to be for peace or are we going to be antiwar? They might have the same result. The issue is, where do we put our efforts, our energy, our integrity? Where do we start to look at our faith? We need to put out the aspect of harmony, whatever this harmony may bring forth, even though it might not look harmonious. Let us have hope. Let it not be false hope, because then we will sit down and think we have done what we needed to do. Then you lose your integrity and others move on while you stand still.

Getting into balance can be quite dangerous when we think, "I made it. So this is it." I have never come to the end of a road without immediately encountering another road. I have never finished a day without encountering a new day. How I work with each day depends upon my level of integrity. Am I going to act according to my opinions, or am I going to act out of the craving for integrity, for my own inner truth?

Are we blind, are we fooling ourselves because we do not want to see all the things that are involved? If we only want to see the light, we become satisfied when we perceive it within ourselves. Many of these things are wishful thinking: "If we put this out, it must be okay." Continuous action is needed when seeking inner truth.

Sadness, to some extent, is a cover for joy; joy often becomes a cover for sadness. Yes, we need to be emotional, keeping the energy in motion. We cannot sit still or stop.

Integrity needs to be on your mind the whole day. If it is not on your mind for one second, then it is also not in your body during that one second. You fail to function as you set out to. Diseases, whether they are diseases of the world, a race, or belief system, show that you are not at ease. They are the result of stagnation, of you not grasping the purpose of the changes being made. We, who think we know, become righteous about what we think others should have already learned and know!

Coming into this new decade, lots of people found their freedom. Look how the same freedom that we were so enthusiastic about, is already in the process of impairment and stagnation. Conditions are being set upon it. Yes, we became physically free. But are we free internally? Are our souls free? Or are we becoming even more opinionated and self-righteous?

We have a right to be free; however, how often do we recognize that with this right, we also have the responsibility to share this freedom with whoever we come into contact with? We attract others looking for this same freedom. The freedom of beingness, not just the freedom to say whatever comes into our minds. There has to be an inner censor. Quite often, we let things out without recognizing our integrity. Sometimes our actions and statements produce the opposite of what we really intended. We act too hastily, impulsively, which is not the same as spontaneously.

Whatever you do, ask yourself, "From where does it come? How was I influenced by what I observed in my environment? How much can I stand up for my own knowingness?" In this society of humans, there are many differences. They need to be there. However, instead of recognizing these differences and noting them, we try to adapt ourselves to the states of other people. This does not work. You are not true to your own self. The differences are there to show you that you are unique. You need to appreciate those differences in other people, so that you can say with your heart, "Yes, I want to be in that particular state. I want to move on so that I can allow the whole universe to benefit from my changes." Then you will not say it is "too good to be true."

Whenever I hear the word "good," I cringe inside. What I call good, I just may not find to be good. It is a matter of questioning ourselves about our values and not portraying this "goodness" as if it were some kind of a great gift which comes to and from us.

We need to share the gift of our own inner goodness. When we get elevated, we need to bring others up to this elevation by showing it and acting upon it. Bring back a harmonious state, no matter what you think or have knowledge of. Bring it back no matter how you were influenced by the outer environment, the news, your relatives, or by total strangers. Ask yourself for that inner statement and stick with it. Allow that inner statement to come forward, through you, your actions, your being, and through your own healing process. It is through healing yourself that you heal the world and begin to converge, although in this state, we are still not totally integrated. There are still too many differences which have not been brought to solution, to flow without hitting obstacles. The obstacles will not suddenly disappear. We often set up obstacles because we want others to think, feel, and act the same way we do. I agree that this seems to be a religious act. If you agree with each other, then it seems you can set up a doctrine and a dogma for the rest of the world saying, "You have to do it this way because we have found this to be. Since there are more than three who agree, it must be so."

In saying, "too good to be true," we question the truth, which is the first act of doubt. Not only do I now doubt my capacity, I doubt my human ability to bring out what I am perceiving. That is *my* doubt, too, by *my* doubt keeps me alert so that I do not drop my attention from it. I keep my mind on what still needs to be done, never becoming too satisfied with my actions. We have done a lot, but not yet enough.

In the inner silence, we find our own inner truth, different from others' truth, but we have the capacity to converge and become a universal truth and to radiate that truth. I do not doubt the availability of the truth nor do I doubt the capacity to bring it out. I sometimes doubt my understanding of what is there and how to bring it forth into the world without prejudice, without self-righteousness. In every opinion brought out is a flavor of self-righteousness, particularly if the opinion is to be accepted and acknowledged by other people.

76

I do not expect nor hope that you take everything I say to become your truth. Every time I make a statement, I too have to question it. That is how I feel but it does not mean you have to feel that way. I do not sway you in any direction but your own.

Whenever my little candle flickers up, it should spark to give your candle the opportunity to flicker up, too. If you would rather allow it to function a different way, that is your right. Please, take the consequences and responsibility for your actions. For too long we have lived in a world that threatened, "If you don't do it this or that way then this or that is going to happen!" We need to work on this every second of our life, using all the things that happen during the night as well as the day. We must set ourselves free from everything that interferes with our knowing and with how our divine self directs us.

I do not always succeed either. Together, on the path toward peace and harmony, we will find the way to understand what integrity means. Be willing to drop opinions if the inner self, the heart, says, "That is not so." How many of us are still making a tremendous effort just to be accepted, to be liked? Learn to speak the truth, show your true colors. If you disagree with something, say it is inappropriate for you to be involved in it. Dare to stand up. Yes, there may be people who like or dislike you, who want or do not want to associate with you. Remember that your higher self is more important than being liked. No matter what you stand for, you are loved. This knowing comes only when you dare measure your love of self, because your higher self is the representation of all love. This love is the love of God you were created from. You were created for the purpose of bringing forth that love. Our purpose is not to be liked or disliked. It is dishonest to yourself to do things to be liked. It is very hard sometimes to speak and live your truth. It will sometimes remove you from those you would like to be with.

It is fascinating to look back at the many times those you felt you could never reach were the ones who stood up for you and were there when you were in need. You thought you had done something to make them dislike you. In reality, they may never have been able to verbalize or show you they appreciated that you took a stand and stated your truth. We can indeed state that "too good to be true" is only a fantasy we sometimes hang on to. We need to continuously work toward an integral process.

Do not wait for the planets to come together to create a harmonic convergence so that you have an excuse to sit on top of a mountain to catch it. If I am a bit nasty about it, that is the true feeling I have. Harmonic convergence, integrity within yourself, needs to take place every moment of the day!

78

Integrity is harmonic convergence. Be a living testimony, so that your energy, your integrity, continues to have an effect upon everything in the universe. To me, that is the greatest promise. The more I become harmonious, integral, in the state of convergence with everything, the more I recognize that things equal to me do not converge that well. They need to be of an opposite nature to create the power to move on. Whatever your disagreements are, they can be the source and power behind improvement in any relationship. We need to look at our acts. The time for talk is over. It is time to act.

DISCUSSION

Question:

Think back to the Persian Gulf crisis of 1990–1991. What can we do?

Answer:

You can show by your actions and deeds that you are there in your heart. I hear in your question a feeling of incompetence, because you could not be there also. Secondly, I hear some guilt. Guilt is more detrimental. When you send out a ray of light with just a little particle of guilt, it diminishes the whole ray of light. Guilt is very destructive. It impairs one.

There is nothing against you envisioning yourself being in the Gulf and contributing. The news you get is a stimulation for you to do even more, but do not feel that you have not done enough. We will never do enough.

Make sure all your senses are involved in your perceptualization. You want to be there; you can be there any time. I can march, even feel the movement of my body. If I can, you can. You need to put power behind your perceptualizations. Turn off your parking lights and turn your heart beam on. Your whole body needs to be involved. You need to feel it, rather than just hear the words. Feeling the words stirs things up within you. You will accomplish something when the energy is in motion. Allow the energy to be emotional.

Perceive peace and harmony without becoming emotional about it. Merely say, "I want peace and harmony." This needs power behind it. When I want it, I need to supply it. You can be anywhere you want even if your body does not get there. This is the marvel of science. Every day we see tremendous advances being made in technology. Recognize the similarities between ourselves and the telephone. In seconds, one thought spoken into the telephone is heard over the ocean without being connected by any wires or by any physical structures. If you have an equal, powerful receptor over there, resonance takes place.

Everything is already in our bodies, but we need to turn on a switch to perceive it in its proper way. Your body is the transmitter and receiver, the antenna. It is your mind that travels, not your body. Even if you are not physically there, they will get the message. This is why you can contribute even if you are not there. Enlighten their minds and fill their hearts with the power of your creative love. In your meditation ask this be done to yourself rather than to them. Because, to me, that means them. The more I live it, the more they will get it. Saying they need it more sounds and feels like being self-righteous.

At each moment you have to know what is most important for you to do. There is no reason that you cannot wash your dishes here and march there at the same time, thereby giving them your strength and support. The more joy you get from washing, the more joy they get from you.

Question:

What exercises link the mind and body?

Answer:

Knowing and knowledge are two totally different things. Knowledge is experienced knowingness. Until you experience knowingness, knowledge has absolutely no worth. You will know everything about everything, but you will know nothing of how it is. If we predominately go by knowledge as presented by others, we do not experience that knowledge, nor do we pay attention to what we experienced.

80

Like a cuckoo clock, a little door opens up and the cuckoo comes out and says, "Cuckoo." When I observe you, while doing this lesson, I observe that little heart saying cuckoo. Yes, I feel that, I know that. It is what people call the "Ah hah, I got it," when you feel experienced confirmation. It is acknowledging that I know what you are talking about. I could never explain it to you, but I know what you are talking about. I feel it. I am experiencing it. This is when the mind begins regulating your body. You feel good when you confirm yourself by yourself.

You need to learn that the intellect should never be the *source* of your information. It is the vehicle to *express* your knowing. That is why we fail. When we look at brain waves of people who are constantly thinking, "Is it right? Is it wrong? Should I, should I not? Yes, but he, she, it, where did . . . " What am I doing now? Doubting! I have another word for it, a much more sophisticated word: deliberating, meaning imprisoning it. I do not let it go.

What am I imprisoning? The energy! In my book, *It's Not What You Eat But What Eats You*, I show that the western brain easily compares to American penal institutions. Both are overcrowded and have no sanitation. The brain is where racism first beings. You force your zinc to be together with your vanadium, your vanadium together with your palladium, your palladium with your potassium, and your potassium with your calcium, all in the same bunch. You cannot move, even if you want to, because everyone is crowded in. This is your first toxicity.

Whatever happens to you mentally, you need to respond to it spontaneously, from knowing. Even when you know you may not have knowledge of it. The rest of the world say, "Ha, that is not so." Well, to them it is not so. That is the risk you take. Here again, you may not be liked for it but you will become nonattached to that also.

Question:

What do I do when I feel inadequate?

Answer:

When I was a visiting minister in a Lutheran Church I was asked if I believed in reincarnation. I heard coming out of my mouth the word "No," which made me more acceptable to them because they did not believe in it either. Then I immediately gave them the bomb. I said, "But I also must tell you I do not believe in God, either." Now just imagine! There I was standing in the pulpit of a Lutheran Church saying that I do not believe in God. I explained that I do not need to believe in God. I *know* that God is and what God represents. Beliefs can be changed. Believing in God, you see, is someone else's interpretation of what God is. The only way to ever know God is by experiencing God.

I do not believe in angels, because I know they are there. I am experiencing them. So it does not matter if they exist or not. Of course, I have my own perception of what angels represent or what they are. This might not fit in with what others have said or written. There are many ascended masters right among us, who have temporarily taken another name and profession. You may think a university professor knows more than a garbage collector. But it is not what a person's physical status is, but what that person knows from his soul experiences. All of you have angelic qualities and you all came here to bring and radiate light. That is why you were created out of light, to bring light.

I have moments of loneliness but I am never alone. I have never felt that I was alone. It is the misinterpretation of aloneness that makes people feel alone. Loneliness comes only when the physical presence is not there. My inner knowing always knows that I cannot be alone. How could I be alone when I am floating somewhere in the universe? I am in it and of it. Therefore, I am one with all of you because we are all of the same substance.

We are not all of the same function. Yet we all interrelate with each other. You know I can walk away from you, but I can never let go of your energy. I exist out of your energy, as you exist out of my energy. This is what is meant when we say, "We are all God's children." We are God and Goddess. I do not say, "I am God." I say, "*God!* am I." I am that creative force upon which I need to act. The more I act upon, the more I become aware of the oneness there.

You see to me, "alone" is "a," "l," then I add another "l," representing God: All One. Alone means "all one." Therefore, I never feel aloneness as a sadness. I feel it as a joy. When we lose connection during the process of being, by our misinterpretation of the situation, loneliness occurs.

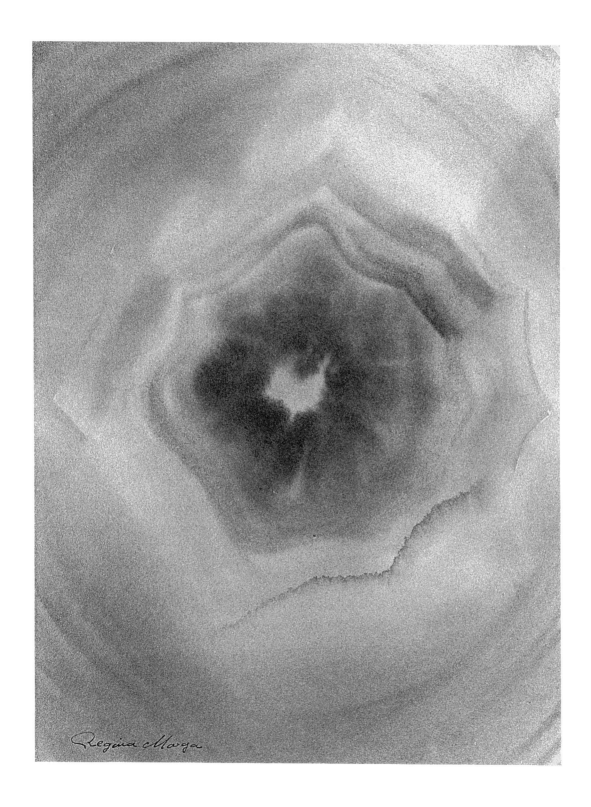

Regina Maga

COMPASSION

I want to fill my heart this world,
　　　Its every suffering and need unfurled.
As from the creative force it whirled,
　　　Into my soul it will awake.
The truth to know what is at stake,
　　　Finding compassion for humankind.
The creative loving power of will and mind,
　　　Delving into life's upper realms to find,
Their light and truth.

　　　Down to earth's deepest suffering descend,
Up to its highest compassion ascend.
　　　Out to its utmost joyful end,
For me, forsooth.

· 14 ·

MAKE NO COMPARISON

MAKE NO COMPARISON. WHAT DO WE MEAN BY THAT? What should we not make a comparison of? It does not mean we should not make any comparison. We need make no comparison of each other. We do not always express what is really going on within us, so it is very hard to compare. Comparison denies our understanding of our uniqueness.

In the world today, we are all actually on trial. We have the right to our own opinions. We have the right to feel. There is an awakening of a form of anger in all of us. I think the anger should not be directed outward toward the world. This anger should be directed inside. We must recognize that this anger is stirring us up to understand where we have been and where we did not express the compassionate state.

Now is the time to start looking within our own self. How much compassion do we have? How much, especially for our own self, not just the outside world? How much of our own being do we still deny? When we attempt to bring light forth from within ourselves, it can only be disturbed by those issues we have not yet dealt with and resolved. We can say that every moment of our life is judgment day.

How much is each one of us involved in portraying the compassionate state? The effect you have upon the world depends on the level of compassion that you bring out of yourself. This compassion will dissolve all comparisons and opinions of how things should have been. Start looking at how we can resolve this great quest. Each of us seems to find ourselves in the "right" place to do the "right" thing toward those who oppose us.

It is very easy to sit in judgment. It is already happening within our own families. When we cannot express compassionate love, we are threatened by anger and the fear of what might happen to us. We cannot put it aside, even though it is removed from us. It is right here. The whole universe, the whole world, is in a state of uproar. We cannot simply still it. What can I do? I can only find what I can do if I sit in proper judgment of what I have done and compare that with what I am going to do.

We need to go within to find that inner peace, and also to recognize how we got to that state of inner peace. It is through our faith that we, as people, can do something about our own beingness, not by our opinions, judgments, or perceptions of what is appropriate for others to do. Find within yourselves what is appropriate for you and start doing that. Look at the division taking place within humankind, within family and society in nearly every country. These divisions are caused by making comparisons and judgments. We cannot compare God. We cannot compare what is the same.

There is only one thing that is the same in all of us: our God presence. Our soul existence. Our purpose of beingness. The fulfillment of that beingness will only come forth if we can find within ourselves the harmonious, balanced state. This we will never find unless we stop making comparisons. The only thing that really counts is what I could have done, what I can do now, and what I need to do.

Yes, we need silent prayer. However, we need more than that. Often, we find within ourselves, answers which pertain to us. Then what do we do with them? We advocate them as being the truth, or we act upon them by stating them to be the only thing that needs to be or could be done, by anyone. I think we need to sit in judgment, questioning *ourselves* about our every act. My tongue is getting shorter and shorter because of the many times, at the last moment, I bit the tip so as not to make a statement that would affect others in an inappropriate way.

We are becoming very self-righteous. It has always been clear to me that self-righteousness leads to a feeling of not being at ease with the world or with ourselves. It is that feeling of change that I refer to. We want the world to change, but how much willingness do we find within ourselves to make that change? Self-righteousness comes from making comparisons. "If they had just done this or if they had just acted upon that." You can bite the tip of your tongue off, not state it outwardly, keep it within, and just "pooh pooh" it away. Recognize that you are sitting in judgment.

What is this judgment based upon? What you proclaim to be your helplessness. The things that press upon us from the outside world are becoming more intense, more dense. This gives us the opportunity to increase our own power to find the power within. Do not look for power from the outside because that power is overwhelming us. Like an avalanche, it comes rolling over us. Do you want to be stuck in that avalanche, or do you want what lies beyond it?

Let us put some vision into the rainbow by taking care of it now. We need to take the judgment of self in a very serious manner, constantly checking our actions. Have I done the same as yesterday? If so, then I have not grown and have also held back the growth of the world. Only through our inner growth will the world be able to grow to the state we all desire, a total renewal of all. We need to take responsibility for the situation as it occurs today, not sit and wait for others to fix it for us.

Total up in your mind all the costs. Why not check what it costs you today? What does it cost you of your nightly rest or of your daily environment? How many times were you stagnant in your work because you were affected by all that was happening around you? Sometimes sadness and pain occurs. Recognize it is touching you. It is touching each of us very deeply. We must not go out in this world stating our opinions without proving we are correct. Instead, we need to give the world an appropriate state of understanding not based on our view of what is good or bad.

Now is the time to look at the compassionate state of that which we all represent; the God self, the inner self that needs to function every second of our life. We all deserve a peaceful night, a peaceful day, and a peaceful life. However, this will not come about by waiting for peace to come to us. It will not come until we activate the inner self, move away from our passions, and transmute them into a higher state. It must come straight from the heart without any consideration if it ought or ought not occur. Then, at least, you will be making an effort to heal yourself and thereby, everything else. It is only through self-healing that this world can be healed. It is not done by going out and trying to heal others. It is already a judgment when you feel they need it more than you do. It is tough. Nearly everyone feels ready to go in and shake them. You need to realize that you are shaking already. Should you not take care of your own shaking before you go out and shake others? Shake them up by how you live your life. Show them you love them.

It seems that everyone has a label for hate. Listen to the children around you. They do not talk about what they do not like; they talk about what they hate. Where do they get this? They get it from adults who constantly express it. Check if your hugs are indeed hugs. Check if your kisses are indeed kisses. Check your commitment to life and those who are living with you. If your pets are suffering, are you expressing turmoil through your beingness? Are you unable to find love within yourself for those who seem to be acting against you? Until now, we felt it in a material way. Are we also aware of how it affects us on an emotional, mental, and especially a spiritual way? The call for awakening is here.

My partner Lois and I just celebrated our anniversary. We celebrated our commitment, not to each other, because that has no meaning, unless I first recognize the commitment to myself, she to herself. I sent her flowers; I sent us flowers. I sent thirteen roses; twelve of them red roses to celebrate each power within ourselves, the twelve powers of life. Twelve roses to vitalize and remind us of the power within which brings forth the commission to love each other under all circumstances. As a finalizing, anchoring force, I added a white rose as an indication of finding the truth of these twelve powers, transcending all the mistakes we made, and starting fresh with a new truth.

We cannot make comparisons with another person. I cannot say, "How did she act in regard to our commitment this last year?" No, my question needs to be, "How did I act upon my commitment in the past year?" Did I apply all twelve powers to the best of my capacity? Did I have the right to look at the white rose as a state of transition? Did I transit? That is the celebration, to be joyful of that which you have achieved. Recognize that there is a whole world open to new discoveries and that you have found the inner communication.

You may say, "Jack, what are you talking about? Why are you so foolish about your anniversary?" It is not my anniversary or her anniversary, it is the world's anniversary. We need to look at the commitments we have made to bring the positive and negative together. This integration portrays love as it is enhanced within this truth. Within this world, we need to begin committing ourselves and seeing everyone as our spouse. We have to marry this world through sickness and through health, for better and for worse, till death do us part. Then we can set ourselves and the other person free, thereby giving birth to a new experience.

89

Check your commitment; only compassionate love can prevail. We need to find freedom for all, freedom for, not freedom from. We cannot do that by making comparisons with others. Where am I today? Where will I be tomorrow? That is where the comparison needs to be. Will I be the same tomorrow? If I am the same, then I have not grown. If tomorrow I am sick when yesterday I was fine, then a change is taking place and I need to take care of it. I cannot compare yesterday and today, or I sit in judgment. I need to look at what I can do to change now.

I have a little dissatisfaction with the way God created us, particularly our form. Of course I am joking but, if I had been God and created people, I would have given them an umbilical cord and immediately after cutting it, I would have put a steel staff in the hole. I would then mount a life-size mirror to look at myself the whole day. To see how I act and react, rather than looking at everyone else. Then I realized God had given me such a mirror. Only, as he has done with so many things, he left a lot of things in this universe invisible. If he had made it visible, you would be so satisfied or dissatisfied with it, you would not pay attention to it anymore. Look at all the things in your daily life you are not thankful for and take for granted. That is why we have to look in the mirror at our own energy.

You cannot tell me that you do not know when you send out light or black clouds. You know how you portray yourself. How much joy, sadness, or sorrow do you spread? How much do you go around every day advocating your misery?

Do we really want to change? Do we really need what is going on in the world in order to change? It seems that we do, because we have not paid much attention yet. Now, at least, we may be starting to learn our lessons. Maybe now we might grab onto the beginning threads of a tangled ball of twine and start to unroll it until we find the end, taking care to observe every part of the twine, so we will know in what direction to go.

DISCUSSION

Whenever we sing the song "Hallelujah" at the end of our fellowship meetings, I feel a tremendous energy being set free. We, who are supposedly giving you a lesson, in reality, are giving a lesson to ourselves. I have always known that I cannot teach anything to anyone. So I feel tremendously elated. I have a feeling of excitement, a very contained excitement. When I have to sing, I realize I cannot contain it any longer. I need to bring it out. Each one of you is actually a part of that. It is swelling up from within and your involvement is practically touchable. This is nonverbal communication.

Computer people have a marvelous statement: "If you put garbage in, you get garbage out." We need to keep our inner being as clean as possible so we do not get garbage coming out. Then our energy pattern will set down what is applicable to us and give it back in a reinforced manner. We will have added something to the situation. I think we always need to ask ourselves whether we can add something to the situation. It is not so important what I say. It is very important to ask myself what I felt, what I experienced.

There is a war about choice going on, on all levels. It strikes me how indignant we are with our choices, trying to pressure other people to make the same ones. I am thinking particularly about the choice women need to make; to carry or not to carry, to abort or not to abort. I am not going to sit in judgment about whether one should or should not. I feel it is very important that we allow each individual to make up their own mind.

We cannot come on with man-made morals and man-made standards. I think it is the judgment of our own conscience we need to start working with. To some extent, we must realize that we go through many abortions in our life. Many of us have aborted good ideas instead of giving life to them. Then we sit in judgment of those who had, for whatever reasons, to do what they had to do. They made their choice. We may or may not agree with their choice. We need to allow people the freedom to make choices. I think that is the strength we have within ourselves. The choice to do what we think is best for ourselves and for all the world. It is not based upon a common judgment or opinion.

A PRAYER

We pray to Thee, O Infinite Guide,
To lift the veil and show the light.
We pray to open our hearts' door,
So we may see an end to all war.
We pray that we may strengthen our faith,
So we may love instead of hate.
We pray to Thee, that we may dare,
To remove our doubts, our truth to share.
We pray to live in peace and harmony,
And to follow thy will, which makes us free.

· 15 ·

THE ANSWER TO EVERY QUESTION

Y OUR PRAYER IS THE ANSWER." I THINK THIS IS SO TRUE. We need to understand what praying is all about. In the first place, recognize the source of our prayer. Form the prayer from your heart. Those desires you ask for from God, you really ask from your own wisdom, your own divine self. God has provided you with all the qualities already in their totality. So we pray to our own God self. Therefore, we can formulate our questions from it. Within prayer lies the answer. I know that when I put something out, the answer is there and will be fulfilled. I do not need to look back and see if it has been fulfilled or not.

A prayer needs to come from deep within yourself. Our friend, Mikhail Naimy, in *The Book of Mirdad*, describes several types of prayer. What we sometimes mistake for prayers are nothing more than requests to God which already have been done but of which we are not yet aware. My prayer, to some extent, is a thank you. Thanking me that I was granted the wisdom to find the question. Ultimately, I will find the answer even if it does not immediately come to me in words. I will see the result from the power I put into it, when I put it out. I put it out in the universal mind, directed by the highest creative force, God. Naimy says:

> You pray in vain when you address yourselves to any other gods but
> your very selves.
> For in you is the power to attract, as in you is the power to repel.

And in you are the things you would attract, as in you are the things you would repel.

For to be able to receive a thing is to be able to bestow it also.

Where there is hunger, there is food. Where there is food, must be hunger, too.

To be afflicted with the pain of hunger is to be able to enjoy the blessing of being filled.

Yea, in the want is the supply of want.

94

Is not the key a warrant for the lock? Is not the lock a warrant for the key? Are not both lock and key a warrant for the door?

Be not in haste to importune the smith each time you lose, or misplace any key. The smith has done his work, and he has done it well; and he must not be asked to do the same work over and again. Do you your work, and let the smith alone; for he, once done with you, has other business to attend. Remove the stench and rubbish from your memory, and you shall surely find the key.

When God the unutterable uttered you forth, He uttered forth Himself in you. Thus you, too, are unutterable.

No fraction of God did He endow you with—for He is infractionable; but with his Godhood entire, indivisible, unspeakable did He endow you all. What greater heritage can you aspire to have? And who, or what, can hinder you from coming thereinto except your own timidity and blindness.

Yet, rather than be grateful for their heritage, and rather than to seek out a way coming thereinto, some men—the blind ingrates!—would make of God, a sort of dumping hole whither to cart their tooth and belly aches, their losses in a trade, their quarrels, their revenges, and their insomnious nights.

While others would have God as their exclusive treasure-house where they expect to find at any time they wished, whatever they did crave of all the tinseled trinkets of this world.

And others still would make of God a sort of personal bookkeeper. He must not only keep an account of what they owe and what others owe them, but must as well collect their debts and always show a fat and handsome balance in their favor.

Aye, many and divers are the tasks that men assign to God. Yet few men seem to think that if, indeed, God were so charged with many tasks, He would perform them all alone and would require no man to goad Him on, or to remind him of his tasks.

Do you remind God of the hours for the sun to rise and for the moon to set?

Do you remind Him of the grain of corn spring to life in yonder field?

Do you remind Him of yon spider spinning His masterful retreat?

Do you remind Him of the fledglings in that sparrow's nest?

Do you remind Him of the countless things that fill this boundless universe?

Why do you press your puny selves all your trifling needs upon His memory?

Are you less favored in His sight than sparrows, corn, and spiders? Why do you not, as they, receive your gifts and go about your labors without ado, without knee-bending, arm-extending, and without peering anxiously into the morrow?

And where is God that you should shout into his ear your whims and vanities, your praise and your plaints? Is He not in you and all about you? Is not His ear much nearer to your mouth than is your tongue to your palate?

And it goes on! But the most important thing brought forth in this passage is the abuse of prayer; to get our requests fulfilled, rather than to sincerely communicate with that older, wiser, all-knowing inner self, that divine self which has the answers.

Go within that heart, as Naimy says, "In a heart does this host assemble." That is where the prayer needs to come from, not just from concocted words in the conscious mind.

One day, just as an experiment, I asked some students if they could give me a prayer. They all sat there and thought and thought and thought. Then finally someone gave a prayer and it was "Our Father," which was beautiful. But you see, it did not come from the heart. It was remembering words, but not the essence from the heart.

You know, we have been walking around lately in a continual state of prayer. We were not even aware of it. We have the desire to make this a better world. We have the desire to overcome all our differences, to live harmoniously. That does not come from your conscious thinking, because your conscious thinking is continuously bombarded with all kinds of things against your desires. Many of us doubt the value of our prayer, because we do not listen sufficiently to our heart.

96

In order to have an appropriate prayer, you need three ingredients. The first is a master desire, a desire of a master. It needs to be a fixation of spirit, a divine discontent. It is God's nature to say this is not the way to do it. That should awaken and ignite the fire within you. This master desire brings up the energy, the fire, which becomes light that we can send out. The words are not important any longer; they are the same as the lyrics to a song. The musical notes are what strike your heart. The words might emphasize the musical notes. So should your prayer, your master desire. Be fixed on it, with nothing else on your mind. Do not think, if it does not work, then I better do this or that. This allows the conscious mind to creep in.

Do you really know if all your prayers were responded to? It might not occur to you until years later you say, "Wow! I did something, I was involved and now I recognize my state of evolution occurred because I was completely involved." I had that divine discontent. I had to be involved in the changes for them to occur. It came from deep in my heart.

The second necessary ingredient comes from that same deep part of the heart. This ingredient is the master thought. It does not come from the conscious mind, but from the divine mind. As spontaneous knowing, it may not have form, letters, or even comprehension to you in your conscious understanding. Your conscious mind drives you to express your divine discontent, your prayer. The second ingredient, the divine thought, master thought, is wisdom expressed. It is not that I have knowledge of it, but I know it. I know it but cannot put it into a form.

The third ingredient is the expression of divine will. Our divine discontent, this shaking in our boots, to our foundations, is awakening us from a time of forgetfulness, not paying attention to and not being involved. This time is over. There is no way you can stay out, you are a part of it. You must do your part.

Notice, this divine discontent stimulates you to do something. If you do not do something, the third and most important ingredient failed or was not activated. This ingredient expresses divine will; make it your own. Listen to that divine will even though your conscious mind says this is ridiculous. "I am doing something for those who are opposing me; I am doing something for those who are ready to make me change out of this physical world. I am going to send love to those who seem to have destroyed everything I love."

It is hard to bring divine will into action. It is a prayer for the "must do"; there is no other way. That power has to be strong enough so that you do not get into a state of stagnation. That light, that desire, comes beaming out. Sometimes at a high level of intent, it fizzles out. This occurs when conscious thoughts question it, not realizing the questions have already been answered. Resonance gives you insight brought in from the world, surrendering your own personal world.

We are like relay stations. The moment we activate that energy beyond our own beings, it comes back to us manifold, not just tenfold. We need to get this world into a better state. Recognize that this is part of our development. As long as we have everything we need, we will start to slumber again. Oh yes, we did, from time to time, put a fire out. We read and sometimes even advocated changes. Then, as soon as we did that, we went back to the way things were before. We were all advising everyone else. We did not follow our own advice. We even became self-righteous about it. We could not understand that these people could not change.

Ask yourself, "Was your prayer strong or was it just an empty request?" Your creativity is the prayer. Every action towards harmony, coming out of the depth of your heart, is the power which will bring a difference. Then we are ready. We are not going to

97

wait for it to be done by anyone else. We are ready ourselves. We start, then, to act out of wisdom rather than just upon knowledge.

I have seen greed over and over. I hear many things which have come to the surface out of the depth of the darkness. What we do not realize, when we put all our attention to the light—praying for light, peace, and harmony—that other forces also come to the surface. They need to come to the surface. Nothing can stay in hiding. All has to come out in the open for an interracial state to exist. Then, no longer will differences exist such as, this is good, this is bad, this is right, and this is wrong. It is all working for one aspect to bring about that harmonious state.

In my perception, that is what prayer needs to be. I do not think you need to bend your knees. You do not need a temple to pray in. The whole world, the whole universe is your temple. You are just an individualized aspect of the temple. If you pray and act upon the insights gained, your temple will become the source, the light tower. It will be affected by any darkness there, still in the process of continuously changing.

What we recognize today as darkness, tomorrow may shine like a star of light. The beauty is that we know we partook of the whole process. We are as much the beneficiary as the one we are directing the light to. It also brings praise to those who pray. So, it is never that you have no result.

Every prayer is to receive the grace which is already there. The answer to every question is to receive the grace of knowing. If we all pray in this way, it will be a different world.

We see a lot happening where real, honest efforts are being made. I think we can help people continue with this honest effort by putting them in our prayers as they put us in theirs. We do not pray for a specific person or a specific group. We pray for all human-kind and for all that have an involvement with life.

Sometimes we seem to feel that humbleness is bending down and denying our own qualities. That is a false modesty. With those beings who are wiser than we are, do not just listen to their words, also observe them in their actions. Observe how they live that energetic pattern, fulfilling their function on earth and in the universe. We cannot limit it to the earth. All the thoughts you send out go whizzing into the universe and bounce back to the place where they need to bounce back. Each of you has your own source of satellites. These are not man-made. Everything you send out will immediately come back, maybe just not to your awareness.

Your prayers need to be pure prayers, coming from the heart. With all that you send out, you have the power to attract and the power to repel. Therefore, what you attract you can repel. You will still attract what you send out. Communication is not one way. Our thoughts and our feelings need to be divinely oriented, coming from our inner being and not from our thinking process, our doubts, or belief systems. Making things whole does not mean unchangeable, for they never stay whole for very long.

We can direct prayers toward continuous change in a harmonious way. We need the chaos, while putting our attention to the order within the chaos. That order is within your heart and soul. There it is never chaotic. That is why your soul will grow, but you might never know it unless you pay attention to it.

Prayer is the answer to every question. Listen, and whatever you hear, send out immediately. If it comes in your feelings, you know you are resonating with your environment.

DISCUSSION

We must realize that the answer to every question is not found by changing others. We must change ourselves and not be affected by things that normally affect us. This is the whole training of nonattachment. You want to be totally involved without being affected by it.

We can scientifically prove it is impossible for anything of a lower nature to affect you. Whenever you lose the sense of excitement, you immediately become sympathetic with that lower input. That is the difference between sympathy and empathy. Immediately bring it up to the heart, instead of saying, "Why is this happening? Everything was just fine, I was in such a great state, now look at what they are doing to me." We rarely recognize that it was us who opened the gate and said, "Come in, come in." That is where nonattachment comes in, in maintaining the flow.

You cannot tell me that you have never had exciting moments in your life, even though you may not be able to portray them. If you cannot pay attention to something which should make you terribly excited, then you need to go back to a former state in which you were excited. Begin reexperiencing that. This will immediately charge the battery up and your light will become bright again. You will then not be affected by anything directed at you.

The Western world is so involved in, and gives so much importance to, the physical aspects of life, that we sometimes have forsaken the fine aspects of life. This does not mean we should not be as busy or give any less value to the material world than we have been doing. We need to apply it in a nonattached way. We may lose friendships because we were not affected by their malfunctioning. You were affected by your good functioning instead of their malfunctioning.

You cannot tell me that it is impossible to have a reason to become excited. It can be something that has happened, is happening, or something that might happen. I perceptualize about twenty-two hours a day. If I am not looking at past movies and replays to get my excitement, then I am creating new ones. I am not only the observer, I am the director, the producer, and the actor. I get into a tremendous state of excitement. I cannot see or perceive any results unless I get into action. I am so busy that anything of a lower nature cannot enter in. It is impossible. I am completely involved with what is happening around me but I am not bothered by it. This is the effort I make.

But I, too, have moments when I do not achieve that level. Then I also have a little lull. I also have some physiological problems. The moment mental problems come, physiological problems come, too. They are interrelated with each other.

Let us say I do not want to hear your question. Even though I do not like the question, I cannot help being put down by it. I say to myself, "If I was not so nonattached, I would get very disturbed with your question." What I am saying, is that I am not that nonattached, because I am disturbed. I need to remind myself to become nonattached. This does not mean ignoring things; that is being detached. Most of us do this. Ignorance is bliss. You fool yourself if you think that, by not paying any attention to what happens around you, you will not be affected by it. You are more affected by it than when you pay attention to it.

You really want to walk the spiritual path, right? So do I, so do most of us. The spiritual path has always been portrayed in such a glorious way. If you walk the spiritual path, you are blessed forever. So many of the thorns are not on the roses anymore. There is nothing that stands in your way. It is just the opposite! The moment you decide to walk the spiritual path, you lose two of your best friends. One you call ignorance and the other you call avoidance.

Once you know something, you cannot make the statement, "Oh, I did not know." You lost your friend, ignorance. When we say, "If you knew, why did you not do anything?" you also lose your friend, avoidance. You need to face everything head on, always counting that you will have the energy and the knowingness to affect the situation without becoming disturbed by it. In my perception, that is the only way to maintain your state of prayer. In my life, it has certainly portrayed itself so. By maintaining my state of excitement, nothing will have an inappropriate effect on me or have power over me. I always come out fine, from the deepest grievance, anger, sadness, and sorrow. I gain new insight.

We need to become futuristic people. We need to start looking at what the result will be if we all work on it. This is why it is not very hard to get excited. As we talk about prayer, I already perceive the world to be in peace. I made a mental film of that. As I watch the film, I keep redirecting. Every time I see a flaw still in it, I put something else in that place, rather than saying, "Well, you know we have to remove this part of it because, as long as they are doing that, there will be no peace." Instead of looking at the goal, look at the result of the goal. Do not look for peace itself; instead, look how peace is being expressed and how it is living in harmony, not just under the label peace.

We have had intervals of that type of peace for a long, long time. For thousands of years we have had wars with intervals of peace. But were we at peace? No, these were acts of temporary tolerance. They do their thing, I do my thing. There is a truce, a cease-fire, but the war continued, flaring up from time to time. There was not really peace and harmony.

Until forty years ago, the country I come from, Holland, was occupied over and over again by foreign invaders. It was once occupied for eighty years by the Spanish, who told us what to do and what not to do. If we look at it, yes, it was a sad state for the people who lived during those eighty years. What has it left behind? It left a piece of country behind which we did not have before. It left a richness of understanding between us and the people who occupied our country.

At the time they occupied our country, we did not make any effort to understand their principles. When everything was settled, we started to gain an understanding of each other. We recognized that, yes, we were different from them. I do not understand why we seem to need to make everyone the same as we are. Only if I was perfect, might I have that wish. However, you know I would not be able to learn anything anymore or have a goal anymore. You might as well start cloning me. We would all become the same. So we need to go beyond intolerance. As I see it, I cannot be affected by it, but I have to do something about it. How can you do something about it? By making sure that you stay different from them. Do not adapt yourself to them or force them to adapt to you.

I cannot tell you how important it is that we recognize our divine unitiés. No one can do your job and no one can fulfill your function in life. You have to do it no matter how many times you have to come back through this school. If you are not ready to graduate, they either send you to a reformatory, which means returning here quickly, or you float back and forth. I have no desire for either of those states, so I might as well do my homework now, while it is facing me.

We have to try to keep our feet upon the spiritual path. We also need to make sure that this foundation does not fall apart. Please keep the foundation, so we can at least create a new blueprint and build a new world upon it. We may not always understand why a particular group was chosen to be the wrecking crew and you the one to build it. Maybe, through prayer, you will get the answer. If you are one of the builders, you make the choice of what your function is.

103

It is not for nothing that your own country, the United States, has the Declaration of Independence. Do you realize that nearly all the people that signed it were builders? It is interesting that they were nearly all members of the Masons. We are all builders, too. We are all cosmic architects and masons. I think we need to build a temple in which all of us can live and express ourselves as creatively as possible. Humankind is waking up! Begin to recognize that you have a responsibility in all this.

INITIATIVE FOR PEACE

With malice toward none,
    With clarity for all,
The initiative gets done,
    Which prevents us from a fall.

With firmness in the right,
    God gives us to see the right.
Upon all darkness let's shine the light,
    Nothing remains hidden, remove the fright.

Let's strive to finish the work we are in,
    The initiative for Peace is about to begin.
To bind up our nations' wounds,
    And restore what's been ruined.

To care for him who shall have borne the battle and
    For his widow and his orphan.
Former negligence abandon,
    Which all may achieve.

The healing of sorrow and grief,
    To cherish a just and lasting peace,
Among ourselves and with all nations,
    Not only for now but for all coming generations.

· 16 ·

INITIATIVE FOR PEACE

T HE INAUGURAL ADDRESS OF ABRAHAM LINCOLN ON 3 MARCH 1865, PERFECTLY FITS THE STATE WE ARE NOW IN.

"With malice toward none, with clarity for all, with firmness in the right and God gives us to see the right, let us strive on to finish the work we are in, to bind up the nation's wounds, to care for him who shall have borne the battle and for his widow and orphan, to do all which may achieve and cherish a just and lasting peace among ourself and for all nations."

In the poem on the previous page, I stretched this out by adding sentences appropriate for today between his lines.

This brings me to the word "initiate or initiative." Initiate: a beginner in a mystery school (schools in which adepts taught the mysteries of life to aspiring students) or similar discipline; one who desires the path of righteousness; the name given to a student until he or she passes the first test. By taking this first step we become an initiate, that is, the one who desires to grow in consciousness and joins a chosen discipline.

The initiative for peace is the chosen discipline. We become an initiate when we make that choice and have the desire to intensify the direction of, or to further our growth in a different direction. When one passes the first test of initiation, they become an initiate. One cannot become an initiate until they go through an initiation. Initiation is the sacred ceremony symbolizing the beginning of a spiritual life.

In an initiation, there are steps designed to test one's mental and physical endurance. One must use their knowledge to keep themselves alive in very painful and frightening situations. At this moment, I think we are going through very painful and frightening situations. We must recognize that now is a time of testing; for us to become initiates and follow the discipline, the initiative for peace.

106

Native Americans go through a process of very difficult, painful mental and physical endurance tests before being fully accepted into the community. These tests illuminate which of their present beliefs come from past karma and life-styles. The initiate can then be reoriented to the beliefs of the community.

When we talk about community, we are talking about the knowingness of the fellowship, not the beliefs of the fellowship. The initiative competes and works through us when we choose to let go of the past. The desire must be big enough to surpass all that we have held on to. Our desire to change needs to surpass the idea that we can do nothing about it.

We do not look beyond the narrow environment of our own cultural state, and so are not in tune with and have ignored far away world situations. In doing this, we do not appreciate others' knowingness, beliefs, and ideas.

I quoted Lincoln's statement so we might recognize that we now have a chance to get the initiative for peace and to follow it up. We must follow up with the work, as Lincoln said, "to do all which may achieve and cherish a just and lasting peace among ourself and for all nations." I feel we need to look forward so that it will be a lasting peace for future generations.

We cannot take care of anyone else's karma. We have to take care of our own karma. Recognize that karma stands for the law of cause and effect. If we are now in a state of uproar and confusion, we must realize we sowed, in the same manner, confusion and uproar. We are now reaping what we sowed. Cause is always followed by the effect. We need to take the initiative, the first step, to bring it into activity. It is time to realize that you are on your way out of this mill.

Have you the desire to take the initiative to walk on a different pathway? A lesser confused pathway? A more extended pathway? A continuous fluctuation of energy displays giving and taking. This is very hard for us to do, even when we are convinced from now on to look at situations in a nonattached way. Suddenly, when news comes which brings pain to us, we are thrown off the path. All our beautiful initiative lies by the wayside. We become totally encrusted with feelings of pain, sorrow, and grief again, because we could not bring about a more beneficial state for ourselves.

Recognize that if you take the initiative, it is the beginning, not the resolving of things, that you encounter. Just taking the initiative will not give results right away. We may have to go through many endurance tests. So do not hang on to the ones you have already gone through and are experiencing at this moment. Deal with them as they come up and then let go.

An author friend of mine, Sid Paulson, reminded me of a poem by Anthony Markham, which asked very penetrating questions. Mr. Markham wrote the poem after seeing the famous painting, "The Man with the Hoe." The poem says,

Who made him dead to rapture and despair, whose breath blew out the light within this brain, is this the thing the Lord God gave, made and gave, to have the meaning of the sea and land, to trace the stars and search the heavens for power, to feel the passion of eternity? Oh masters, lords and rulers in all lands, is this the handiwork you give to God? This monstrous thing distorted with soul crushed? How will you ever straighten up this shape? Touch it again with immortality. Give back the effort, look and the light, rebuild in music and in dream. Make right the immoral, infamous. The fatuous wrongs in medical woes. Oh masters, lords and rulers in our land how will the future reckon with this man? Our answer has but question end hour. Will rulings of rebellions shake the world? Or will it be with Kingdoms and with Kings? With those who shaped him into the things he is, when this dumb terror shall reply to God after the signs of the centuries.

When taking the initiative, we need to do so without question. It is enough to wake up, sit back and look at what we have been partaking in. Why did we not wake up earlier? If we have no answer, let us at least make a decision to wake up now. We must not quell the souls of so many, particularly the soul of this earth.

Let us all make a real commitment to take the initiative for peace for ourselves and all that exist in this world. We will then begin to recuperate from all the things which we have felt were not functioning within ourselves.

Remember that anything you are currently complaining about is actually a mirror for actions of your own malfunctioning. I know that is hard to hear. It is not for you to feel guilty for letting it come so far. By taking the initiative for peace, you need to mirror this in your actions from now on. Take peaceful actions instead of being afraid of vulnerability.

As anthropologist Angeles Arrien states, "The Western world is so afraid of vulnerability that we try to avoid it and fight it." In reality, vulnerability means that you have enough power not to be affected by anything directed toward you. Your power is of a greater state. Until you discover this power within, you cannot serve this world, you cannot lure the light of the world's mirror to you. Become more vulnerable, say yes, instead of sitting and complaining about what is happening.

We need to do something to restore within ourselves all those aspects from which we have been hiding. They could harm and hurt us. We claim to control our pain when, in reality, we have been hiding our pain. We need to be willing to let our pains come forth so we know what our needs are. We can then give that love and need back out to others in need. This will start pointing individuals back to themselves, so there will be no need to hide or avoid vulnerability.

We are living in a dysfunctional world at the moment. We all come from dysfunctional families. You might not like this to be stated so openly, but that is the way I perceive it. Over the last century, there has not been great family togetherness, a functional unit relating with each other not just as relatives by blood, but as relatives of God, children of God. I think it is a very important step we are going through.

Thank you for letting me remind us of the marvelous potential we all have within. We now need, besides all this potential, the courage to begin expressing it. Courage is a gathering of energy to bring out and express. If you still hide your vulnerability, you cannot express your courage. Being vulnerable shows that you are courageous and willing to stand for what you know needs to be done.

109

I believe in Armageddon; however, I do not interpret it as something very tragic. I interpret it as something very beautiful. It means that the world will no longer exist as we have known it over the last several centuries.

Let us be honest, we are not that happy and satisfied with it either. It is time for a new caring culture. The old world will be destroyed. What do we mean by the word "destruction"? Is it destruction to create something new that is beneficial, benevolent? If we use destruction for destruction's sake and then leave it lying around in pieces without doing anything about it, that represents the Armageddon we have all been expecting.

I have said a thousand times over that doomsday was yesterday. The earth today does not look the way it looked yesterday. So the way it was yesterday must have been destroyed in order to show its "today" face. I might not like its new face, but it is up to me to destroy that face again in order to create a new face for tomorrow. This state is an active, progressive state.

You see, Armageddon was looked upon as the beginning of a new era. I know, very strongly, that we went into this new era too early and were not totally prepared for it. We were not finished with the old era. We went unprepared into the new era of the water bearer, Aquarius. If we had stayed agricultural people and never tried to know more about the universe, but just continued to walk behind our plows, we would not have the problems we have today. We would also not have experienced life as abundantly as we have. We would not have had the challenge to use all the new powers we discovered in the universe. We have the choice to use them for the good of all, or to use them again in a destructive way without rebuilding.

110

We have been creating so fast without allowing our conscience to grow and expand at the same pace. Originally, the astronomers had figured out it would take 2,140 years to go through the Piscean age. It began the day of Christ's birth and would last until the year 2,040. In 1973, we went out of the Piscean Age and into the Aquarian Age. Because we moved, changed, and added so much energy to the earth, it caused the earth to move around its own axis much faster. As the earth moved faster, it began to wobble around its own axis, tilting slightly and becoming rounder instead of being pear-shaped. The poles started to become equal, climates started to change.

On top of that we rape mother earth and she now has hormonal changes before going into a new state. She starts having pimples, acne, fluid retention, and, from time to time, contractions which result in tidal waves and severe climatic changes and eruptions. All this happened to the earth because we went so far so fast and were not prepared for the changes.

So now we are going through a struggle. It seems that time is speeding up; actually, time is slowing down. A day off was like a week's vacation. Now when you wake up in the morning, you discover you have to start work in a couple of hours. When the day is done, what have you done? Well, in comparison to what you did two hundred years ago, it seems you have not done anything. In reality, you have done ten times as much. There is a much greater mental involvement now. Consciously or not, you are all involved in making Armageddon come about.

The Aquarian age is the middle age. The Piscean age was the age of enlightenment. It did not necessarily teach us how to use the light. We all had our candles lit and were walking around with them, but we did not really know where we were going. We are now in the area between earth consciousness and God consciousness, moving toward cosmic consciousness. This is why the earth and planetary systems are becoming smaller and closer together. We know more about others and other areas and thus, have a greater understanding of the total universe.

When we become the God conscious, there will be no need to be in these vehicles, these bodies anymore. When all students graduate, there will no longer be a need for school. Earth is a school that comes with a guarantee. The guarantee is that somewhere in the universe is a school with more advanced classes than our current ones. We will be a more collective intelligence, hooked up to and aware of our source. We must start hooking up to the main powerhouse, God consciousness. We have to pay the price. We can no longer just blink at things and act as if we do not need to do anything different or change our way of thinking and doing and being. We have to get to work.

111

Let us now go through a meditation, looking at the points we must take initiative on, to achieve what is right for humankind and for all in this universe.

Take a couple of deep breaths. Allow your eyes to close so you are not diverted by the conceptual world. Stir up some excitement for this magical something that we are. Think of words that will lead you into a new experience. Whenever I read a sentence, see if you can experience it as if *you* are speaking to you. Let the words resound within your minds and bodies. I will use the term "I" to help you experience the words. You are talking to your higher self now.

I am excited about the self-expression of the infinite that I am.

I am enthusiastic and excited about my growing ability to recognize, acknowledge, and express my real potential.

I am excited about my growing confidence and faith in the light of the world that I am.

I am enthusiastic about my growing willingness to individualize the Will of God in all that concerns me.

I am excited about my growing understanding, ability to work with, and knowledge of the light of world.

I am excited about my growing ability to imagine the good available for expression through me.

I am excited about my growing delight in the radiant energy that flows into self-expression as me, through me, and for me.

I praise and give thanks to the Creator of light for the truth and light that I am.

I am enthusiastic about the unsuspected powers of self-expression now coming to light in my consciousness.

I am excited about the new mental, emotional, and physical activities the light inspires in me.

I am excited about the light, the radiant energy, the living flame that consumes every facet of false belief, every negative thought and feeling.

I am enthusiastic and excited about the light of the world that is becoming a personal living experience for me.

Allow these words to work and resonate within you. Measure your vulnerability, realize how sensitive you are becoming and how much you can now direct this energy into your own self-expression.

Envision yourself in the center of a circle with all of us surrounding you.

Envision the rays of your light touching everyone in the circle and immediately start feeling it move from your center outward to the people in the room.

Become aware of the motion; how it goes in a marvelous counterclockwise direction, expanding from beyond that circle into the whole earth, shining upon all those who are in need of your light.

Now exchange places and become part of the circle. Even though we do not touch physical hands, our life touches each other, creating a huge sphere of brilliant light, penetrating into every part of all that is. It has become so subtle that the light activates and energizes all that needs to be energized.

Become aware of what you are perceiving and how it reflects from the outer rim back to your own personality.

Become aware of your own personality starting to merge and integrate with your higher self.

113

I know that you have taken the initiative for peace and have gone through a self-initiation, looking at all the qualifications and all the potentials of the power that is, to bring peace to fulfillment.

Now take a deep breath and release it with a sigh. Again, take a deep breath and release it with a sigh.

I do not know what some of you may have felt. I feel a lot of us are going through a new stage of rebirth. It is as if we too are in a state of pregnancy, as if the light impregnated us. It is like an immaculate conception. We are creating new beings out of ourselves. We are, indeed, having intercourse with God when going through these stages. We know that the right energies are then going to make the new form we need to live. This will make healing easier because we can maintain its wholeness. We do not need to spend as much time trying to put together what was falling apart. We will become more preventative in our actions and use our true morals in the world in all our actions and relationships.

THE WORLD THAT MADE MEN

This is the world that made men.

    These are the powers she did bestow

From her bosom, so we could grow.

    This is the world that made men.

These are her mountains, minerals, and rocks,

    Which give us stability and strength

To maintain for a lifetime at length.

    This is the world that made men.

These are her trees and her plants,

    Which give us examples of seeds, flowers, and fruit

To show progressive creativity, for consciousness, its root.

    This is the world that made men.

These are her fishes, birds, and animals

    Which give us the power of motion and play,

To accentuate our mobility for actions of a wide array.

    This is the world that made men.

Out of her own body it gave to thee,

    All the qualities on Earth to be.

For us to respect, honor, and to Earth be kind,

    To leave the world that men made, forever behind.

WORLD HEALING

ORLD HEALING RELATES TO THE HEALING OF SELF. We are becoming more aware of the importance of change, both of ourselves and of the world.

It was just about a decade ago that James Lovelock, an atmospheric scientist on contract to NASA, observed changes taking place on the earth and in the earth's atmosphere. He found this state to be similar to homeostasis. The earth and its atmosphere maintained a beneficial stability and equilibrium while in this continuously changing state. As changes occurred, coordination and self-regulation took place.

Since we exist within this system, it is an ideal model to observe because world healing relates to healing ourselves. We have, within ourselves, the capacity to produce homeostasis for self-regulation and to create a better world by becoming better self-regulated people.

Irving Golging, an author and friend of James Lovelock, suggested giving this hypothesis a name. He suggested calling it after the Greek goddess, Gaia, who supposedly created earth. In Homer's Ulysses, he describes the universe as not only a "theophany" but also a "cosmogony." Homer states that first there was chaos, fast and dark. Out of this Gaia came forth, the deep-breasted earth. Then came Eros, to soften the hearts, thereby producing the influx of all living things on the planet.

We can see that theophany occurred when, out of darkness, the earth was created. This activity, by itself, brought forth a feeling of eros, a softening of the hearts. It gave forth out of its hardness, its solid substance. It would give forth, in the form of love, its influx which then created all living beings and things.

This does not change the idea we see in all the schools of philosophy and thought, that we were created out of love. That is the fruitful substance which maintains the changes taking place within us as well as on planet earth. Remember, these changes should take place and need to be followed in order to fulfill our own function of having dominion over this earth.

Look at nature whenever changes, disruptions in the normal flow of life, take place. Watch nature restore the flow by itself with its tremendous capacity of diversity which maintains unity. Unity and diversity is the first thing we need to look at. We lost unity because we did not observe the unified aspect of diversity. Everything is interrelated. Our diversity has caused us to be in the state we are in.

How can we do some world healing? First, we need to look at all living things on this earth. Nature has simplified and modeled for us how life comes about and goes through its different stages and levels of consciousness. Whenever we have a seed, we cannot hold on to it, put it away, and then expect something to happen. When we hold back the seed, we hold back all its power, potential, and tremendous capacity to bring forth new life.

We have not recognized the "bringing forth" aspect of the seed. We need to use our thoughts and mental capacity to plant the seeds of our mind within the universe. Recognize that each seed needs to be planted in a suitable environment to bring forth a diversity of fruits. As speakers and teachers, we direct our ideas, "seeds," to the world; that idea or seed functions and grows into a marvelous plant or person. It eventually flowers and gives fruit and then begins expanding again, bringing forth new seeds. In a different environment, philosophy, or school of thought, these seeds take root in the same soil from which they originated. We cannot say that others should treat a seed this way or that way. We need to recognize that each seed must be planted in the soil from which it originates.

Even our geographical state is different from any other geographical area. Scientists say, if we want the greatest benefit from that which the earth brings forth, we need to utilize and eat what is from our immediate environment, our geographical location. By this adaptation, we will return to the homeostatic self-regulating capacity of our environment. We need to recognize the different qualities within the diversity. We treat practically everything as if it had exactly the same qualities and values.

117

Genetically, geography makes us different. For instance, I was born in Holland, several feet below sea level, and have a genetic structure adapted to that particular state and atmosphere. When I came here I had to adapt myself to a different physiology. Therefore, I cannot say, "I do this, so you must do it too; because it is the best thing for me, so it is also best for you to do." I must take into consideration others' original geographical location and genetic structure because it has a memory, too.

We need to adapt ourselves and give. Our thought processes must adapt to the atmospheric state in which we live. We have a much greater capacity to associate ourselves with nature since we are still surrounded by nature. It is much harder for people who live in cities in a tremendously contracted state. If they want a breath of fresh air, they must go to a park or to a street where all the greenery has not been taken away.

To begin healing the earth, we must consider what we put out. To restore the earth to its full growing capacity, we must become more involved in it. There are not that many of us living in this natural environment. We also need to look for ways of healing the earth for people who live in the atmosphere of a man-made structural environment.

How do we put our architectural aspects together? Are they in relationship to how the earth operates, grows, and brings forth its ideas and forms? We must go back to more natural forms and understand how energy moves. It is never a square energy; it is a spiraling energy. It energizes and passes, spiraling, through us. We must fit in with this spiraling energy.

It is interesting to note how we put everything in our environment into square boxes, including our homes. We are then so surprised at being constantly in opposition. We, ourselves, have caused a lot of the opposition, not realizing that it is not a homeostatic capacity to restore it to a more natural form. We even put up edifices in honor of our Western ideas of making everything solid, rather than allowing the spheres to move through free-form.

Even in our language, our verbal communications, we have created a free flow from which we can recognize our faults *as* they come forth from us which affect these faults on the same level, instead of a higher level. We again overlooked unity in diversity. Even though things are diverse, they still partake in a total unity. Therefore, they need to be brought into their own atmosphere and rhythm of life.

One of the most important ways for us to begin healing the world is by restoring our own personal rhythms. We need to adapt ourselves to the rhythm of life. The rhythm of the earth, like a pulsating heart, pulsates within us, too. We adapt ourselves to this from the moment of birth. Just ask the astronauts; the moment they get far beyond the earth, their heart does not beat the same way it did here on earth. We adapt ourselves to our environment. Look at how the ills of the world are nearly all caused when we become arrhythmic with our environment. We did not understand or follow the flow.

In the course I teach on breathing, we use techniques adapted for our Western beingness to restore rhythm. We start listening inside to our own beingness. Your inner rhythm gives you an indication of what the rhythm of your environment is at that moment. It is up to us. I feel part of our domain is to restore whatever needs restoring. Realize what kind of disturbance we are creating at this moment all over the world. Let's make it rhythmic instead of trying to adapt ourselves to an irregular rhythm which becomes more difficult to overcome.

Let us restore the world to its peaceful, harmonious state. We must adapt ourselves to our own rhythms in order to adapt them to the rhythms of the earth. By restoring both our rhythm and the earth's rhythm, we adapt to the diversity of the earth, and relations between all things on the earth will become rhythmic again with our own being. Whatever you are at odds with, comes from an arrhythmic state. People not on the same wavelength and not operating with the same power, have different frequencies. Frequencies are the cycles we use to measure time, man-made time.

Just ask yourself how many times you muttered about something not flowing the way you wanted it to, and how you wanted to change "it" instead of changing and adapting yourself to the flow. The other side was not in rhythm with you, so you wanted it to change rather than changing yourself.

The philosophy of nonattachment is a pathway toward healing the world. We can say, "We are involved and recognize all the arrhythmic things but are not disturbed by them," as we maintain, increase, and adapt our rhythm to the universe. By doing this, we get results rather than saying, "I cannot deal with that because they do not want to change the way I want them to change." We must recognize that the world can only be made whole and healed again if individuals all start to relate as unique beings.

Ask yourself, "What is my intent? Do I want to become high and spiritual?" Recognize that it must be put into practice. Your intent must show in the actions of your daily life, not just in words, prayers, or acts done for the approval of the outside world.

Every step you take needs to be taken for the sake of making this a better world and making you a better person. Recognize the rights we have so that they override what we seem to be fighting for. Recognize that consequences mean responsibility, the ability to respond to those rights. We must look at freedom "for" rather than freedom "from." This will start healing the world. It is just a step we take on the path. We need to measure every step we take by asking ourselves whether we have brought out all our potentials. Did I do it for the "I" self so that I would eventually be recognized as a great world-changer, or did I do it to change the world? Am I trying to change my fellow beings by giving in to their needs and forsaking my own?

We came here fully functional, making it possible to maintain dominion over this beautiful world. Mother Earth gives us opportunities to grow, over and over again. At this period in time we are being given another opportunity. We may not like the teachers, lessons, or the methods in which the lessons come. I think that is your right. If your dislike becomes so strong, do something about the lesson and not to those who bring the lesson. I feel that is a very important part. We are creating a feeling that we must go against those who give us the lessons.

120   I remember from school that I did not particularly like the methods by which they taught me certain things. I did not think I would ever use them in my life. I even disliked the person who taught me. The methods they taught were against my own method and feeling. Now I look back and I see I am utilizing many of those things which, at that time, under hardship and pressure, I was forced to learn.

It is interesting that, if we want to heal this world, first we need to work toward healing the education system we created and make it educational again. We need to make it "bring forth" rather than "push in," stimulating everyone to feel and sense for themselves; teaching everyone to bring metaphorical images out into an expression of life. Stir the capacity of creativity. Become an integral being who uses analog in a digital capacity instead of a digital person.

I have a dislike for people who claim to be very artistic and creative and say that anything to do with logistics is bad. This is the same thing as one who always thinks logically and proclaims that all metaphorical stuff and creativity are not worth the paper they are written on. That person is one-sided and has forgotten the bipolar aspect of the universe.

It is because of bipolarity, the positive and negative, that we have diversity and unity. This process restores the homeostasis of the whole world, inclusive of ourselves. We each need to adapt it to ourselves in our personal case. We do not spend enough time and understanding on what is happening with us throughout the world.

Emphasizing suffering in the world is not doing any good. We need to really start looking for that inner power within ourselves to work these things out. All of us have some trauma, whether we know it or not. I was convinced that I could self-regulate myself, that my past war traumas would not bother me anymore. Well, I was shown differently. During the Gulf War I was bothered. My task now is to understand what I must do in order to transcend that trauma; not to get rid of the trauma, but to understand what I learned from it.

Every day we must look at our own beingness and not make fast statements or solutions expecting other people to change. It would be very easy for me to hope that the sirens and bombs will not go off anymore. It would be nice, but it would not help me never to have another trauma recurrence; I would not have dealt with it yet. I would just be hanging up a big shield, my roadblock that states "ignorance is blind, ignorance is bliss."

Every day we are confronted with situations in our relationships that show us that even though we may have done our best, our best was not good enough. We still have to work harder on it. The only way the world will ever be healed is for each of us to stop taking our task so lightly and to fulfill our capacity to transcend the things that have happened since conception. Do not blame, feel guilt, shame, or doubt.

We need to keep our own energy field output as high as possible. We must become more radiant so we will not be affected by lower vibrations. The moment we give power to anything, our energy goes down. The lesson I learned from the Gulf War is that I, again, gave power to the bombing and killing. When I gave it power over my actions, I became powerless; not only with less power but *powerless*. That is my insight: to know that I have to keep myself in the highest possible state.

Our intent is to maintain peace. The power of our intention, our motivation, will always be stronger and no lesser energy can penetrate it. This is my strong belief. If it were not so, there would be no reason to become as radiant as we can be. To me that is the only power which is pure God power. There is no power higher than pure white light. As long as we keep that in mind we do not need to be concerned about what others do. I cannot perceive anything that can penetrate this tremendous capacity we have to portray and surround ourselves with pure white light.

Whatever we put around anything, has to come from within us. The light I protect myself with, comes from within, not from without. As it flows in from the universe, I immediately allow it to flow through and I become as radiant as possible. I do not think there is any higher power in the whole universe than pure God power. It comes in as truth. Any situation we are still affected by contains a lesson we have yet to learn. To increase the power, it must come from within, not by asking, "*Why* did I do this or that?" but instead by asking, "*How* am I affected by it?" To be affected by it, I must have dropped my own level of consciousness.

We install so much fear in people, by constantly seeing the endangering factors in the universe. This does not allow people to see that there is only danger when we do not fulfill our function. If we fulfill our function, there are no dangers. There is nothing stronger than this power of divine love; knowing that your soul is one with all. Your soul cannot be assaulted or insulted. The only thing that can be insulted or assaulted is your body. When your soul is strongly developed, you have the advantage of your soul energy. It will not be as quickly affected, if at all. The vehicle through which you operate will give its full power. You spend so much energy on holding back. I do not want this vehicle to hold back anything. If this means flying in space, then into space it is going to go. There is no law that can keep it down.

You cannot evolve unless you involve. Work on self means allowing the lower self to adapt to the higher self with the motivation of providing the world with its higher need. It is my motivation that I want to become very, very radiant so that I can shine upon those in need. With this direction, this motivation, I work on myself.

Note by the artist, Regina Marga

Seeking more individual expression throughout a foreign language teaching career, I returned to my love of watercolor painting. Local landscapes took form. But not until I joined Jack Schwarz and Aletheia as an intern did I really tap tools to access my creative intuition. Spontaneous expression of energy in motion revealed new patterns of light and color reflecting a mirror of awareness to me. It is with deep love, gratitude and joy that I now join these images to Jack's expression.

For further information and tools for study on Jack Schwarz and Aletheia contact:

THE ALETHEIA FOUNDATION

515 N.E. 8th Street

Grants Pass, Oregon 97526

(503) 488-0709